Forgotten Chi

Child's Birthday card, 1915 (author's collection)

First Published 2014

Introduction

All non-fiction books require a great deal of careful and accurate research and over the past ten years, it seems that I've spent an inordinate amount of time hunched over a microfiche reader in reference libraries and family study centres countrywide. Yet it seemed that no matter where I was or what subject I was researching, one name seemed to pop up over and over again - Margaret Ellen Nally[1], more usually known as Maggie.

Eventually, finding myself with a little spare time on my hands, I decided to see what I could find out about Maggie, who was cruelly murdered in London on Easter Sunday 1915, the day after her seventh birthday. I immediately hit a brick wall. The size of newspapers in general was much reduced during the First World War and the main focus of the limited column space was reporting on the hostilities. Maggie had the misfortune to be murdered only a few weeks before the first air raid on London took place. She was also killed just two weeks after the arrest of the 'Brides in the Bath' murderer George Joseph Smith, who was charged with drowning three women, after marrying them bigamously and then quickly despatching them for their life savings. Thus with the newspapers of the day dominated by news of foreign battles and the impending trial of Smith at the Old Bailey, which began on 22 June and ended with a guilty verdict on 1 July, very few column inches in either the national or the local newspapers were devoted to a little girl who was brutally raped then asphyxiated with the piece of cloth she had been given by her mother to use as a makeshift handkerchief, before being dumped in a ladies' lavatory at Aldersgate Street Station (now Barbican.)

Yet what little information that was available about Maggie's death proved very interesting as I discovered that three more children were murdered between 1908 and 1915 and that all four murders remain unsolved. Many people believed at the time that Marie Ellen

Bailes (1908), Winifred Baker (1912), William Starchfield (1914) and Margaret Ellen Nally (1915) were killed by the same person. Sadly, almost one hundred years after Maggie's murder, it is a matter of pure conjecture to try and determine what happened to all four victims and it is now highly unlikely that the truth about these tragedies will ever be revealed.

I have tried to piece together the stories behind the children's deaths using information from the contemporary newspapers, as well as more recent research, the sources of which are listed at the end of the book. However, much as today, not everything that was reported in the press is entirely accurate and there were frequent discrepancies between different publications. Where there is a direct conflict of information between sources, I have included an explanatory footnote but otherwise I have stuck with the most commonly quoted variant.

Every effort has been made to clear copyright; however my apologies to anyone I may have inadvertently missed. I can assure you it was not deliberate but an oversight on my part.

I must thank several people who helped me bring this project to fruition. These include Ana Ramos, who conducted research in the British Library on my behalf. John Hughes is a descendant of the Nally family and was extremely generous with his time and with sharing information about his ancestors. He and Tim Stygall very kindly allowed me to use their family photographs as illustrations, as did the eBay seller, who wished to remain anonymous, but permitted me to use his auction photograph of a penny-in-the-slot toilet door lock.

Viv Head of the British Transport Police History Group was also exceptionally helpful, both in checking his society's records for information and also for supplying some current photographs of Barbican Station at a moment's notice. Christine Matthews also permitted me to use one of her photographs of Maggie's father's place of work.

My husband Richard supplied me with a seemingly bottomless mug of tea whenever I disappeared into my office to write for hours on end. He also proofread this account and made many helpful suggestions and, as always, I am enormously grateful for his input and support.

As we mark the centenary of the commencement of the First World War, and commemorate those who gave their lives for their country, it seems a particularly appropriate time to spare a thought for innocent victims Maggie, Willie, Winnie and Marie, who died not as a result of the hostilities but whose lives were cruelly cut short by a person or persons unknown. Their stories deserve to be told...

1 There is some dispute about Maggie's middle name. Her birth certificate indicates that she was registered as Margaret Helen Nally, whereas her death certificate clearly shows Margaret Ellen Nally. Without exception, every newspaper report of the case uses Margaret Ellen, so I have chosen to use that version throughout this account.

'Maggie was the dearest little kiddie God ever put breath into...'

Although Britain and Germany had been at war since August 1914, by April of the following year, almost all of the fighting had taken place on the battlefields of Europe. The first air raid on the United Kingdom happened on 19 January 1915, when Zeppelin air ships dropped bombs on King's Lynn and Great Yarmouth in Norfolk. However, at that time, London was still out of range of the Zeppelins and hence the capital did not experience the first of its many air raids until 31 May 1915, when seven people were killed and a further thirty-five were injured [2].

Maggie Nally, courtesy of John Hughes

Even though she had uncles fighting in France, the hostilities were of little concern to Margaret Ellen Nally, known affectionately to her family as Maggie. The little girl, who was a pupil at All Angels' School in Cirencester Street, Paddington, celebrated her seventh birthday on Saturday 3 April 1915 and the following day, which was Easter Sunday, began at 8.30 a.m. with a breakfast of bread and butter. Like most children on such occasions, Maggie spent much of the morning stuffing herself with sweets and chocolate. Yet although she had eaten an Easter egg and some caramels, she was still ready for her lunch of stewed giblets and mutton with potatoes, which she ate with her parents and three siblings at 1.30 p.m.

After lunch, Maggie begged her mother to let her visit her grandfather and other relatives so that she could tell them all about her birthday. Maggie's relatives lived in and around Carlisle Street, Marylebone (now Penfold Street), which was roughly a thirty minute walk from her home in Amberley Road, Paddington. Even though she was only young, Maggie had made the walk alone before, although she was more usually accompanied by her brothers, nine-year-old Sydney [3] and four-year-old John Patrick. However, on this occasion Maggie went to Carlisle Street by herself, leaving home at 3.30 p.m.

Dressed in her Sunday best with a pink ribbon bow in her hair, she wore a grey coat with a brown half collar, two metal buttons and two side pockets, with black socks and nearly new black button boots with patent leather toes and a blue-grey felt hat, trimmed with tiny yellow artificial flower buds [4] and green leaves, held in place by a sturdy band of elastic under her chin. Under her coat she wore a white pinafore, tied with a bright flowered sash, over a dark red dress with a pearl button at the back and two petticoats. Maggie's mother, Bessie Christine Nally (known as Christine) watched her daughter as she met up with two neighbouring children in the street, who walked part of the way to Carlisle Street with her.

Maggie arrived at Carlisle Street at 4.00 p.m. and went straight to the home of Betsy Scott, whose husband Frederick Donald Scott was away fighting at the front. Although Betsy wasn't strictly a relation, her daughter, Lena Betsy Scott, had married Maggie's father's brother, Arthur Lawrence Nally [5], so Maggie called Betsy 'Auntie'. Betsy had just returned from taking Lena's baby to Maggie's grandfather's house and asked Maggie if she was on her way to see him.

Maggie asked Betsy's four-year-old daughter Alice Rose Marie Scott if she would go with her to see her grandfather but the little girl refused, saying she had only just come back from there and adding that John Nally, who she called 'granddad', had given her a penny [6]. Having visited her grandfather, at around 5.15 p.m., Maggie dropped in to see her uncle at his home on Richmond Street, a soldier whose name is recorded in the contemporary newspapers only as Private Hoare [7]. She left after a few minutes, telling Hoare that she was going to Mrs Scott's house. On her way back, she went to her grandfather's house again, where she popped her head around the door to ask if her father [8] was there. John Nally told her that he wasn't. He gave his granddaughter a halfpenny for her birthday present and Maggie continued on to Mrs Scott's.

Maggie spent the rest of the afternoon playing out on the street with Alice. At around 7.30 p.m., Alice's mother asked the two girls to run an errand, sending them with a message to a neighbour. When they returned to Betsy Scott's house, she sent them out again to a nearby shop to buy some safety matches. After coming back with the matches, Maggie and Alice began to play the piano but Mrs Scott had a headache and was feeling unwell, so the sound of two young children banging noisily and tunelessly on the piano was too much to bear and she gave them a penny to go and buy sweets. Alice came back alone at around 8.00 p.m. and when Betsy asked her daughter where Maggie was, the little girl replied 'Gone home', pointing down Carlisle Street in the direction of Church Street and also towards John Nally's house, which was around two hundred yards away [9].

Hyde Park Mansions, 2010. © Christine Matthews.

By kind permission of Christine Matthews

Meanwhile, Maggie's father had also been in that neighbourhood himself that afternoon and had last seen his daughter at 4.30 p.m., when she was playing with Alice on the corner of Carlisle Street and Richmond Street. John Henry Nally [10] then went home to snatch a little sleep, before reporting for a night shift at Hyde Park Mansions, Chapel Street, Marylebone, where he worked as a caretaker, porter and lift operator. However, he was woken up at 7.00 p.m. by his wife, who told him that Maggie had not yet come home. He reassured her that their daughter was probably still with one of her aunts or her grandfather but Christine was not convinced. Maggie was normally a most reliable child, who was always home before dark and never stayed out beyond 6.00 p.m., or 6.30 p.m. at the very latest. (Although Betsy Scott was certain of the timing of Maggie's movements that evening, which were also corroborated by Emily Knight, the niece of the owner of the shop where the two girls bought the matches, the fact that Maggie didn't leave Carlisle Street until around 8.15 p.m. seems a little at odds with her parents' insistence that she was always home by 6.30 p.m.)

At his wife's urging, John Henry set out to walk to Carlisle Street, following in reverse his daughter's most likely route home, along Formosa Street, Shirland Road and Blomfield Road into Maida Vale and through Lyons Mews. On reaching Carlisle Street, John Henry spoke to his father, who confirmed that Maggie had left for home a short while earlier. However John Nally was convinced that his granddaughter would have taken a completely different route, walking down Church Street, along Edgware Road and Maida Vale, down Clifton Road into Warwick Avenue and from there into Formosa Street. Unaware that Maggie had still not arrived home and thinking that he had simply missed her en route, John Henry went straight on to work to do his shift.

Meanwhile, growing ever more worried as time passed, Christine desperately walked the streets in her own search for her daughter, reporting her missing at Paddington Green, Harrow Road and John Street Police Stations and contacting Paddington Infirmary in case her child had met with some sort of accident.

However, Maggie seemed to have disappeared from the face of the earth and when there was still no sign of her by 10.00 p.m., Christine went to her husband's workplace to let him know that their daughter was still missing. John Henry suggested that Christine should go and ask her relatives if they had seen the little girl, telling her that she should then go home and see if Maggie had turned up while she was out. Nobody had seen any sign of Maggie, so Christine waited anxiously with her two sons and youngest daughter, Ellen, hoping and praying that Maggie would walk through the door. At 1.30 a.m., she could stand the wait no longer and went back to Hyde Park Mansions to fetch her husband. John Henry Nally left work and went straight home with his wife but almost as soon as they got there, the police were knocking at the door with news of their missing daughter. Sadly, it was the most tragic news that any parent could ever hear.

2. There are wide variations between different publications in the reported numbers of dead and injured in the first air raid on London. Some sources state that the death toll was as high as twenty-eight.

3. Sydney was registered at birth as Sydney Thomas Walker Lawson, which was his mother's maiden name. He was born in 1906 and Christine Lawson didn't marry John Henry Nally until 1908. Although he was known as Sydney Nally, it is not clear whether John Henry Nally was Sydney's biological father hence he is either a full or half brother to Maggie.

4. Some reports state that the hat Maggie was wearing was dark blue rather than blue- grey and was decorated with 'ball-like' artificial white flowers.

5. Arthur Lawrence Nally married Lena Betsy Scott in 1914. A member of the 8th Battalion King's Royal Rifle Corps, Rifleman Arthur died on the field of battle in France in March 1918.

6. Some reports suggest that Alice agreed to accompany Maggie back to John Nally's house and the two little girls went there together.

7. Although he is not fully identified in the contemporary newspapers, 'Private Hoare' is assumed to be John Hoare, who married John Henry Nally's sister Mary Elizabeth Nally in 1909. By 1915, they had three children, Catherine, John and Edward. John Hoare served in the Rifle Brigade.

8. Some newspapers report that Maggie asked her grandfather if her uncle was there, rather than her father.

9. Whenever Maggie visited Carlisle Street, she often referred to her grandfather's house as 'home'. Hence, when she told Alice that she was 'going home' it is not clear whether she was intending to return to her home in Amberley Road or was planning to go back to her grandfather's house.

10. To distinguish him from John Nally (his father and Maggie's grandfather) Maggie's father, John Henry Nally, will be referred to as John Henry throughout.

'To think that Saturday was her birthday and now she is dead.'

Aldersgate Street Station (author's collection)

Sixty-year-old Metropolitan Railway Inspector Richard Charles Groves went on duty at Aldersgate Street Station [11] at 7.00 p.m. on 4 April 1915. His first task was to make a full tour of the station, including the ladies' and gents' waiting rooms and lavatories, during which he observed nothing out of the ordinary. It being Easter Sunday, the station was quieter than usual and there were very few people around, although Groves later estimated that more than thirty-six passengers passed through the station between 10.30 p.m. and midnight.

After the last train of the night pulled out of the station at 11.51 p.m., Groves extinguished the lights on the platform and, by the light of a hand lamp, made a final tour of inspection of the entire station, locking up as he went. Everything seemed as normal, until Groves reached the ladies' waiting room. There was usually a female attendant present but she had left at 7.00 p.m., so the facilities had been unattended since then.

The ladies' waiting room looked fine but when Groves checked the adjoining lavatory he immediately noticed something amiss. There were two separate compartments, each of which contained a water closet and Groves saw that the right-hand cubicle was 'Engaged', the door shut and locked, so that anyone wishing to exit that lavatory would have been forced to climb over the partition and leave through the door of the adjoining compartment [12]. When knocking on the lavatory door and calling out produced no response, Groves opened the penny-in-the-slot lock with his pass key but found the door obstructed from within. Groves pushed hard at the door and forced it open sufficiently to put his head into the cubicle and, to his horror, he saw the body of a little girl lying on her back with her right cheek facing downwards, her feet pointing towards the door, her arms outstretched, her hands open and palm upwards and what was described in the contemporary newspaper reports as 'a piece of her clothing' (presumably her knickers) lying across her legs. The child's mouth was open and Groves could see something discoloured inside it, which protruded slightly beyond her lips. He immediately realised that the little girl had been raped and murdered and sent for the police, attempting unsuccessfully to revive her with artificial respiration while waiting for them to arrive.

Her still warm body was taken to the mortuary at Golden Lane, where she was examined by Divisional Police Surgeon James Kearney, who estimated the time of her death to be around 10.00 p.m. The discoloured item inside the child's mouth proved to be a piece of piqué or ribbed cotton material, which was stained with blood. (It was variously described in the contemporary newspapers as being white, off white or dark brown with a black stripe running through it.) Kearney believed that the 11" x 9" strip of material had once formed either the lining of a man's waistcoat or an undershirt, tapering into a point where it once fitted the shoulder. The cloth was not starched and its edges were rough and jagged, as if it had been hurriedly torn from a garment, probably with the sole purpose of stifling the child's screams.

Knowing that a little girl fitting the description of the dead child had already been reported missing, the police went to Amberley Road and escorted John Henry Nally to the mortuary, where he identified his daughter's body. The following morning, Maggie's grieving parents made statements to *The Daily Mirror*:

Christine and John Henry Nally, by kind permission of John Hughes

'Maggie was the dearest little kiddie God ever put breath into' sobbed a distraught Christine Nally. 'She had bright blue eyes and brown curly hair. It was a terrible blow to me. She was a girl who would not make friends easily and I cannot understand how anyone could have enticed her away because I had always warned her about following or going with strange men and I am sure she would do what I had told her to do. I do not think he could have carried her away, because she was a big, sturdy child. It is awful. I cannot believe that she has met such a death. It must be a maniac who has done it. To think that Saturday was her birthday and now she is dead.'

'How she got to Aldersgate is an awful mystery to us. I cannot understand it at all' continued John Henry Nally. 'Maggie went over to Marylebone, which is quite close to us, to her grandfather on Sunday evening. She was last seen playing about in Carlisle Street at a quarter-past-eight. Since that time she was not seen by anyone until they found her at Aldersgate Street. We were searching nearly all the night for her.'

'London's Best Detectives Employed' read the headlines in *The Daily Mail* of 6 April 1915, informing its readers that officers from both the City Police force and Scotland Yard had been brought in to investigate the murder. Initially, the police were confident of solving the crime and finding the person responsible for Maggie's death very quickly. They announced that they had lifted several fingerprints from the waiting room and the toilet door lock but detectives saw the piece of material in the child's mouth as their most important clue, believing it to have been hastily torn from her killer's clothing to serve as a makeshift gag. However, this supposition was quickly dashed when Christine Nally told them that she had given the piece of cloth to Maggie to use as a handkerchief before she left home and within days the police also announced that the finger print evidence garnered from the waiting room and lavatory had proved useless.

In the immediate aftermath of the discovery of the body, the police made a thorough search of the ladies' waiting room and discovered a halfpenny on the floor, which they speculated might have been given to Maggie by her killer to entice her away. The police believed that Maggie had dropped the coin while trying to fight off her attacker but seem to have ignored the possibility that it was actually the halfpenny given to her by her grandfather for her birthday. Maggie was known to keep her 'handkerchief' in her coat pocket and could conceivably have placed her grandfather's gift in the same pocket, to fall unnoticed onto the floor when the cloth was snatched from her. Additionally, Betsy Scott gave Maggie and Alice a penny and Alice later told her mother that, whereas she had bought sweets, Maggie kept her halfpenny share of the money.

Because of Christine Nally's insistence that Maggie would never have gone off with a strange man there was initial speculation that she might have been abducted by a man dressed in woman's clothing but this theory was quickly discounted due to the extent of the shocking injuries to the child's sexual organs and also the fact that a woman dressed in long skirts would doubtless have struggled to climb over the partition to escape from the locked lavatory cubicle.

Maggie was last seen on the corner of Carlisle Street and Edgware Road, roughly half a mile from Edgware Road Station. The police were confident that her killer took her to Aldersgate Street Station by train, reasoning that to get to the ladies' waiting room from the street outside the station, whoever killed Maggie would have needed to approach the ticket collector at the gate with the child in tow, have their tickets punched then continue to the waiting room, always in full sight of the ticket collector. However, if the man and child arrived at Aldersgate Street by train, they would automatically pass the ladies' waiting room on exiting the station and it would be relatively easy to duck inside, particularly if the abductor was aware that there was no attendant on duty on Sunday evenings. Not only that but the murderer could then exit the station alone or return straight back to the platforms and make good his escape by taking a train going either east or west. The police questioned whether or not the murder may have been committed on the train or elsewhere and the body dumped in the lavatory but decided that this was highly improbable, since it would have involved openly carrying the dead body of the child possibly on to, but at least off the train, through the station and up the stairs. Having accepted that Edgware Road, Farringdon Street, King's Cross, Euston Square, Portland Road (now Great Portland Street) or Baker Street Stations were the most likely starting points for Maggie's final journey, the police concentrated their house-to-house enquiries in the area of Carlisle Street and the half-mile long Edgware Road. Every stall holder, publican, café and restaurant owner in the neighbourhoods of Edgware Road, Euston Road and King's Cross was questioned about their recollection of their customers on 4 April and the police appealed in the newspapers, asking the public to report any possible sightings of the murdered child between Westbourne Park and Aldersgate Street Stations.

11. Aldersgate Street Station was renamed Barbican in 1968.

12. This was obviously a deliberate action by the killer to buy time before Maggie's body was discovered. Because the toilets were operated by 'penny-in-the-slot' door lock, the mere action of closing the compartment door would ensure that the door was locked. However, the display window would read 'Vacant', meaning that the door could be opened by the very next person to insert their penny. By locking the door from the inside and climbing out over the partition wall, the killer ensured that the door lock read 'Engaged', which would have led people to believe that there was someone inside and discouraged them from trying to access that particular cubicle.

'Some of these persons were obviously mistaken'.

Barbican Station, 2013, (formerly Aldersgate Street Station)

By kind permission of Viv Head, British Transport Police History Group

The newspaper appeals brought forth a flood of information from well-meaning members of the public, all completely sincere in their beliefs that they had seen Maggie in the hours leading up to her death. These included a woman who was absolutely certain that she had seen Maggie on the south side of the river Thames, a sighting which was quickly dismissed because it simply didn't fit with what was definitely known about Maggie's movements and the doctors' estimates of the time of her death.

A policeman on duty outside Aldersgate Street Station on 4 April claimed to have heard the sound of a gunshot at around the time of the arrival of the last train. It was questioned whether whoever killed

Maggie had been so overcome with remorse that he immediately committed suicide by shooting himself. However the gunshot - If indeed there was one - was later ruled irrelevant to the enquiry, especially when a search of the railway lines from Faringdon Street Station in one direction, to Moorgate Street Station in the other, revealed no physical evidence and no suicides were reported in the area. A special constable told investigating officers that he had seen a man running out of Aldersgate Street Station at around 10.00 p.m. but was unable to describe him.

One of the first real clues came from Alice Scott, who told a neighbour that when she left Maggie in the street, she walked off with 'an old man.' Although Alice was too young to give any further description, her statement was given added credence by Mrs Walker, the keeper of a shop in Burne Street - a continuation of Carlisle Street, located close to Edgware Road Station. Mrs Walker, who lived almost opposite the station, recalled that on Sunday evening she looked out of her window and saw an old man giving what she described as 'pudding' to some children in the street. She went out and warned the children not to take anything from the old man, who told her 'Oh, it is quite good and I will not do them any harm.'

Having seen Maggie's photograph in the newspaper, Mrs Walker was positive that she came into her shop in Burne Street on Sunday evening and bought a bag of sweets, known as 'cream mixtures'. She was unable to say at exactly what time Maggie visited the shop, apart from knowing that it was definitely in the evening and she told the police that she hadn't seen any men about at that time, old or otherwise.

However the significance of Mrs Walker's evidence is difficult to gauge because of confusing and apparently conflicting newspaper reports. When the initial results came back from pathologist Bernard Spilsbury's examination of Maggie's body , it was suggested that she had eaten some kind of meal shortly before her death consisting of '…remnants of meat to which hair was attached'. Although it was impossible to determine at that early stage precisely what the meat was without further analysis , Spilsbury felt that the most likely candidates were pig's trotter, canned meat or brawn, a traditional British dish made from the meat from a pig's head, cooked, jellied and eaten cold. There were three shops in the immediate vicinity of Carlisle Street that sold brawn, but only one, owned by a Mr Walker, stayed open later than 7.00 p.m. on 4 April. Police visited Walker's shop in Burne Street and took away samples of canned meat and brawn for further analysis.

Walker was interviewed by the press and stated that his shop was open until midnight on Easter Sunday and was very busy indeed. 'So many people, grown-ups and children, passed in and out of the shop that I had not time to notice one more than another' said Walker, although he did recall that his customers included 'countless children' and a number of soldiers.

Although both shops were on Burne Street, it is not clear whether Mr Walker's brawn shop and Mrs Walker's sweet shop are one and the same establishment, or even whether Mr Walker and Mrs Walker are related. Yet after Mrs Walker's assertion that Maggie bought sweets from her shop appeared in newspapers from 6 April, it was subsequently reported in the newspapers dated 9 April that 'Mrs Walker cannot remember selling anything to a soldier or a little girl like Maggie Nally on Sunday night.'

A publican contacted the police about a group of soldiers who were drinking in his pub on Edgware Road at around 8.00 p.m. When one was refused service because he was drunk, he parted from his companions and left the pub alone. Police were also told about a well-dressed woman wearing furs, who was said to have been offering sweets to little girls in Carlisle Street on 4 April. When the woman realised that her behaviour was attracting attention, she laughingly remarked 'It is all right. I only fell in love with one of the children's lovely hair.'

An Italian family from Duncan Terrace, Islington, reported that on Good Friday, two days before Maggie's murder, their eleven-year-old daughter was sent out to fetch a newspaper and was approached by a man offering to take her to the cinema. When the girl refused, the man asked her to walk with him to the tube station, saying that he was meeting his sister there. The man led the terrified child towards the station, where she managed to escape from him, running all the way home. She later described the man as '...being of medium height, clean shaven, with very fresh complexion and dark hair. He was dressed in a black coat and dark trousers with a tweed cap.'

On the day before the murder, two children were approached by a man who tried to persuade them to go with him by offering to show them some postcards. The children ran away but were able to describe the man as '...of short stature, of dark complexion and dressed in dark clothes and a check cap'. Significantly, these children were accosted in Edgware Road and last saw the man standing on the corner of Carlisle Street, in almost exactly the same spot where Maggie was last seen alive.

Other children in the area stated that they too had recently been spoken to by a man in a check cap, all of them describing him as '...well over middle age'. The police were inundated with complaints of 'strange men' molesting children in the streets, including ten-year-old Mary Wallace from Burne Street, who claimed to have been offered picture postcards by a man, who then grabbed her arm and tried to pull her into a side street. Mary was with her older sister at the time and managed to break free from his clutches and run away. The girls described the man as short with a very pale face and large eyes and maintained that they had later seen him following other little girls.

In the course of their investigations, the police interviewed every single railway official who was on duty on 4 April, from both the Metropolitan and District Railways. Among them was Edward Spencer, a porter at Aldersgate Street Station.

Spencer recalled seeing a respectably dressed woman accompanied by a child in the booking hall at some time between 7.00 pm and 8.00 p.m. on 4 April. (It should be remembered that Maggie was reportedly last seen in Carlisle Street at around 8.00 p.m.) Spencer was taken to the mortuary to view Maggie's body but could not identify her as the child he had seen. He also reported seeing a strange man loitering near the ladies' cloakroom some six or seven weeks earlier. There had been recent attempts made to force the locks on the toilet doors to get at the pennies within and Spencer formed the impression that the man was after the money and informed an Inspector. The man ran away when approached and Spencer remembered him as being thirty-two to thirty-four years old and about 5' 7" tall, with dark hair and moustache and a thin face. He apparently looked like a builder's labourer and wore a grey overcoat, a muffler and a black cloth cap.

Station employee Frederick George Cook told the police that he had seen a woman and child going into the ladies' waiting room at about 7.00 p.m. on the night of the murder, although again this was before Maggie supposedly left her relatives on Carlisle Street. A Metropolitan Railway guard was in charge of the train from Hammersmith, which arrived at Aldersgate Street Station at 9.45 p.m. on 4 April, having called at Edgware Road at approximately 9.32 p.m. There didn't seem to be any passengers disembarking at Aldersgate Street and the guard was about to give the signal for the train to leave the station when he heard a door handle being repeatedly pulled, as if somebody were struggling to get out of one of the rear carriages. He went to assist but before he could get there, the carriage door opened and a woman and child alighted from the train and walked towards the station exit, a route which would have taken them past the ladies' lavatory where Maggie's body was found. The guard described the woman as '...of respectable working class', saying that she was between thirty and thirty-five years old, around 5' 3" tall and dressed in dark clothing, with a dark, flat hat. The little girl accompanying her had wavy hair and was not wearing a hat, although she had a light coloured ribbon bow on the side of her head. The guard recalled that the child was wearing a coat, beneath which he caught a glimpse of something white, most probably a pinafore.

'I particularly noticed the child' he told the police 'as she was looking towards the train and was not wearing a hat'. The guard further stated that he did not know at which station the woman and girl boarded the train but, on being taken to view Maggie's body at the mortuary, was positive that she was the child he had seen. Yet, although the guard claimed to be absolutely certain that he had seen Maggie with a woman, the statements made by other station staff did not corroborate his recollections. A porter recalled closing the carriage door before the train pulled out of the station but did not remember seeing a woman and child. The assistant guard remembered seeing a woman getting out of the train but did not think that she was accompanied by a child.

On 9 April, police released the news that someone had confessed to Maggie's murder. In a cinema in Dover, a soldier told an attendant [13] that he was responsible for killing Maggie and, when the police were called, he repeated his confession to a constable. The man was Eugene McGann, who joined the East Kent Regiment, known as 'the Buffs', in February 1915. After going absent without leave from his regiment, McGann was arrested at Ashford on 7 April 1915 and detained at Dover but managed to elude his guards and went to the cinema. Having confessed to the murder, McGann was taken to the police station, where he clammed up, refusing to give any further details of his movements on 4 April, while still continuing to insist that he was Maggie's killer.

The City of London Police asked their colleagues in Dover to investigate McGann's movements and a detective was sent from London to interview him. It was quickly established that McGann had actually been in detention and under close supervision on 4 April and so could not possibly have committed the murder. The police also discovered that McGann had previously handed himself in to police in London some years earlier, falsely claiming to have murdered another child by cutting her throat, when no murder had actually taken place.

McGann, who was known to be a heavy drinker, was described by the newspapers as '...someone whose speech and conduct showed that his condition generally was not normal'. He was eventually handed back to his regiment and was medically discharged from the Army on 28 May 1915 on the grounds that he was, '...not likely to make an efficient soldier'. Newspapers explained to their readers that such false confessions by soldiers were particularly commonplace in wartime, either because the men had become delusional due to their horrific experiences of fighting or because they wished to avoid or delay being sent to the front lines. Indeed, one soldier serving in France reportedly falsely confessed to murder, in the hope of being sent home to Britain for trial.

Having discredited McGann's confession, the police also had to deal with what they later described as 'a cruel hoax'. A train ticket from Royal Oak to Moorgate Street Station dated 3 April was found, on which somebody had written the words 'I intend to kill a child to-night' [14]. Although the ticket was dated the day before the murder, the police could not ignore the possibility that it was written on later, although they eventually came to the conclusion that the words were written by '...a foolish person, who hoped to introduce further complications into an already complicated case.'

The most promising lead of all came from bus conductor Edward Redman (or Reedman), who was convinced that Maggie had ridden on his bus in the company of a soldier. According to Redman, the soldier and child boarded his bus outside Gardiner's shop in Chapel Street, Edgware Road between 8.15 and 8.20 p.m. on 4 April and got off at King's Cross twenty minutes later. (Chapel Street is within a few hundred yards of the place where Maggie and Alice supposedly parted company for the last time. It is also the location of the block of flats where John Henry Nally was employed.) The bus conductor was taken to view Maggie's body at the mortuary and had no doubts whatsoever that she was the child he had seen with the soldier.

He recalled Maggie as being aged between six and eight years old and 'healthy looking', with a round face and stated that she was wearing a dark grey coat and no hat, adding that she was 'snivelling'.

As Redman's bus pulled up at the bus stop at Chapel Street, he was about to step off onto the pavement when the soldier pushed the child forward. Redman asked him to let those passengers wishing to leave the bus get off first and the soldier replied 'All right, sonny.'

London Bus, 1910, showing the open top deck (author's collection)

As Redman stood next to the soldier, waiting for people to get off the bus, he came to the conclusion that the man was 'half dazed', most probably drunk. The conductor also thought that the little girl seemed very timid and gained the impression that she really didn't want to be with her companion. When they eventually got onto the bus, the little girl hesitated on the platform as if to go inside but the soldier grasped her sleeve and pushed her firmly up the steps, saying as he did 'Up you go.'

He and the girl sat on the back seat and when the conductor went up to collect fares, he asked the soldier where he was going to but the man took no notice of him. Redman said that the man was holding his head down and appeared very dozy. When the conductor pressed him for money, the soldier eventually responded by asking him 'Where do you go?'

'It's not where we go to but where you want to go' replied Redman and, after thinking for a few seconds, the soldier asked 'Do you go to the Cross [King's Cross]?'

'Yes, that will be 1½d each' confirmed Redman.

'All right' replied the soldier handing over a shilling and Redman gave him the two tickets, which the soldier promptly gave to the little girl to hold, before pocketing his 9d change.

It seemed strange to Redman that a soldier should be out so late with a young child, especially when he heard the soldier roughly tell the snivelling girl to 'Shut up.'

'Has she lost her hat?' Redman asked the soldier curiously.

'Oh, I don't know' snapped the soldier dismissively.

In an effort to soothe the clearly distressed little girl, Redman took a paper bag of dried figs out of his pocket and offered it to her. She didn't take one, so Redman selected the largest and handed it to her, although she just held it in her hand and the conductor didn't see her actually eating it.

The soldier and little girl got off the bus at King's Cross, at the corner of Gray's Inn Road. Redman saw the soldier take hold of the little girl's sleeve again and propel her towards the Great Northern Railway Station. They then stopped in front of a whelk stall, where Redman lost sight of them as his bus pulled away.

Redman was able to give the police a very detailed description of the soldier, who was dressed in a full khaki uniform, including a greatcoat. The soldier's uniform was described as being 'rough and dirty', with no flashes on the shoulders to indicate which regiment he belonged to and no cap badge. Instead, in the place where the cap badge should have been, were some numbers or letters written in indelible pencil. The man was about thirty years old and 5' 8 or 9" tall. He looked ill and had a very sallow complexion, brown hair, a short light brown moustache and around three days' growth of whiskers on a 'medium face'. His boots were very muddy and he appeared either dazed or drunk.

The conductor recalled that there were three other passengers on the top of the bus at the time – a young man and woman, probably a courting couple, who were sitting together and a man who, according to Redman, '...looked like a railway goods porter'. The police remained sceptical about the conductor's alleged sighting of Maggie Nally. According to Redman, the child and soldier got off the bus at 8.40 p.m. and, had they then gone by train to Aldersgate Station, the journey would have taken only a few minutes. Since the police surgeon put the time of Maggie's death at 10.00 p.m., if it was Maggie on the bus, nobody could fathom where she had been between 8.40 and 10.00 p.m. Mr Burwick, the owner of the whelk stall at King's Cross, was interviewed and told the police that he had no recollection of seeing a soldier with a child on the night of 4 April. Furthermore, the police had always assumed from the outset that whoever lured Maggie away had done so with kindness, a theory that seemed at odds with the soldier snapping angrily at the snivelling child and ordering her to shut up, which seemed more in keeping with the behaviour of a harsh father. Finally, nobody could understand why, if the child were Maggie Nally -

described by all who knew her as 'bright' and 'intelligent' - and she was being taken somewhere against her will, she had not spoken out and asked the friendly conductor for help.

Redman's statement was printed in the newspapers and police appealed for the soldier and the other passengers to come forward, even if only to be eliminated from their enquiries. They also asked for any witnesses who had seen any soldiers with children on 4 April to contact them and the appeal was read by stagehand Mr James of Holloway, who worked in a theatre in the West End.

The bus conductor's description of the soldier in the press reminded James that he too had seen a similar man at King's Cross tube station on the night of 4 April. ' I particularly noticed that his badge was missing from his cap and that some figures or words were written in the place of it' recalled James. 'This fact and his dejected appearance caused me to look at him closely'.

The soldier was holding his head down but happened to glance up and see James studying him intently. According to James, the soldier gave him an indignant look, as if to say 'What are you looking at me like that for?' before turning his face away. Unfortunately, for the police, whereas the stagehand's description of the soldier was almost identical to that of the bus conductor, James was adamant that he saw no little girl with, or even anywhere near the man, who became known in the investigation as 'the dejected soldier'.

By the ninth day after the murder, the fifty or sixty police officers who had worked continuously on the case since the very first were no closer to making an arrest. They revealed that they had resorted to disguising themselves and following suspects and stated that every district of London had been carefully watched and anyone upon whom the slightest suspicion had fallen had been closely questioned. Several men had been taken in to various police stations for further questioning but all were able to satisfy the police that they were not involved in the murder and were later released without charge. Shocked, appalled and no doubt frightened for the safety of their children, Londoners were understandably keen for the murder to be solved and the police received what they described as 'shoals of letters' from the public. Detective Superintendent Ottway (or Ottaway) and Detective Inspectors Willis and Thompson had to deal with baskets full, the majority of which contained nothing more than theories, speculation or even dreams and were therefore valueless. People became frustrated at the apparent lack of progress in the case but the detectives pointed out that every single lead generated had to be properly followed up. 'Each statement made, whether it takes the detectives to South Croydon or Palmer's Green or West Kensington has to be investigated and the public who are not aware of the methods of the police are inclined to grumble at the lack of news of likely clues' commented a police spokesman, adding that while detectives were extremely grateful for all the help they had received from the public, they urged people not to try and play at being amateur sleuths.

No importance was attached to the statement of a witness who believed he saw Maggie Nally at a cinema in the King's Cross area, although the timing of his sighting was consistent with the bus conductor's evidence of when Maggie and the soldier got off the bus. 'If the murderer reached King's Cross at about 8.40 p.m. and visited a picture theatre, the strong presumption is that he would have remained there till an hour which would have made it impossible for him to reach Aldersgate Street by 10.00 p.m., the time fixed for the crime by doctors' responded a police spokesman, adding that they had questioned staff at several cinemas, without finding anyone who had seen Maggie. However, on 14 April, the newspapers reported that Maggie's missing hat was believed to have been seen in a cinema.

The breakthrough came as a result of a letter received by the police. It was written by a soldier, who was on leave in London on the night of the murder and visited The Grand Cinema in Edgware Road, within a quarter of a mile of where Maggie parted company with Alice Scott. In front of the soldier were two empty seats and on one of them lay a child's hat, matching the description of Maggie's headgear. The soldier told the police that he picked the hat up and wore it as a joke for roughly ten minutes, before skimming it across the cinema to some girls, who were sitting close by.

The entire cinema was thoroughly searched but no trace of the hat was found, nor did any of the staff remember seeing it. Then a woman came forward to say that she had seen a dog playing with a similar hat in Earl Street, near to the cinema and that area was also searched without success. A child's hat was found in Regent's Park but when it was shown to Christine Nally, she was certain that it did not belong to Maggie. The police renewed their appeals for anyone with information about the hat to communicate with them and confirmed that they had sourced a replica, which they had placed on Maggie's head at the mortuary as an aid to identification for those potential witnesses viewing her body.

The search for the missing hat became one of the main strands of the investigation. The police questioned whether the murderer might have taken it and, indeed, we now know that many murderers take personal items (or even body parts) belonging to their victims as a trophy - a tangible souvenir that allows them to relive their murderous experiences long after the event (Douglas, 2010). Back in 1915, police were baffled by the fact that the hat was missing and initially questioned whether Maggie was even wearing it when she left home. 'It is not unknown for children of this class to go out without hats' commented one police spokesman but after Maggie's parents and other relatives insisted that she was wearing a hat that afternoon and that she still had it on when she left Betsy Scott's home for the last time, the police concluded that '...for some unaccountable reason', the murderer may have taken it away with him.

'A madman would be likely to do such a thing' speculated the reporter in a *Sunday Post Special* of 11 April 1915 'whereas neither a maniac or a sane person who had committed a murder on the impulse of momentary madness would be likely to throw it [the hat] away while taking the child to the scene of the crime or carry it away for the purpose of flinging it into the canal. Left beside her body, the hat would have told the police less than the piece of cloth found in the child's mouth and the only additional theory that the police can form is that the child may have been taken to some house previous to the train journey to Aldersgate Street, where she was murdered. The loss of the hat, without a doubt, forms a mystery within a mystery, which it is difficult to elucidate.'

13. Some accounts state that McGann originally confessed to the person he was sitting next to in the cinema, who reported what he had heard to the attendant, who immediately fetched a police constable.

14. Some newspapers report the words on the ticket as 'I intend to kill a girl to-night'

'On the face of it, the case appears to have been a cruel and atrocious murder...'

The inquest on Maggie Nally's death was opened by coroner Dr Frederick Joseph Waldo on 8 April 1915. Waldo had recently been elected as President of the Coroner's Society and such was the public interest in the case that large crowds assembled at the entrance to the City Coroner's Court to watch the arrival of Maggie's family, as well as the Assistant Commissioner of the City Police (Captain Bremner), Home Office Pathologist Dr Bernard Spilsbury, solicitor Mr E. H. Rawlings (representing The Metropolitan Railway), Divisional Police Surgeon Dr Kearney, Detective Superintendent Ottway and Inspectors Thompson and Willis.

Waldo opened the inquest by outlining the known facts of the case for the jury, explaining perhaps unnecessarily 'On the face of it, the case appears to have been a cruel and atrocious murder'. The coroner mentioned that he intended to have Maggie's body placed in 'the preserving apparatus' at the mortuary for as long as her parents would permit him to, in order to give anyone else who might have information relevant to the investigation the chance to view her body.

The first witness was John Henry Nally, who related the events leading up to his visit to the mortuary to identify the body during the early hours of 5 April. He identified a bundle of clothes, some of which were visibly blood stained, as having belonged to his daughter. As Nally carefully examined each little garment, his wife sobbed loudly and rocked backwards and forwards in her seat in a frenzy of grief. Other women in the court were also visibly affected and a friend sitting near to Christine tried unsuccessfully to comfort her. Nally also assured the coroner that he personally had not been to Aldersgate Street Station for almost ten years and said that he had given a comprehensive account of his movements on 4 April to the police, who were fully satisfied that he could not possibly have been involved with his daughter's murder.

When Christine took the witness box, she was almost totally overcome with emotion and broke down several times as she described what she knew of her eldest daughter's last few hours. She confirmed that Maggie had never complained about anyone accosting her or offering her sweets and insisted that Maggie would not have gone off with a stranger. She also confirmed that Maggie had no problems with her eyesight and would therefore not have mistaken a stranger for somebody else.

When Christine was shown the piece of material removed from her daughter's mouth she broke down completely and sobbed uncontrollably for several minutes. Eventually a glass of water was handed to her and she was able to confirm that the cloth had once been part of a baby's cape, which was subsequently made into an overall and that she had given it to her daughter to use as a handkerchief before Maggie left home for the final time. However, when Christine was asked to examine her daughter's clothes she gave way to a tremendous outpouring of grief, bordering on a total collapse.

'Oh, I cannot, I cannot. Not that; not that. No, no!' she sobbed hysterically 'It is terrible, terrible.'

She turned to run from the witness box but her husband restrained her, trying gently but firmly to persuade her to stay and answer Superintendent Ottway's questions.

'You beast! To suggest such a thing to a mother. To torture a mother like this is terrible' she screamed at the police officer, as he persisted in trying to show her Maggie's undergarments, which were described as 'very much torn.' Christine eventually recovered her composure sufficiently to answer the Superintendent's last few questions, before being allowed to step down.

Betsy Scott detailed Maggie's movements during the afternoon and evening of 4 April then it was the turn of Station Inspector Richard Groves to give his evidence. He described the quietness of the station, telling the inquest that he spent the hour between 11.00 p.m. and midnight on the platforms attending to trains. He confirmed that he didn't see anybody - man or woman- who was accompanied by a little girl during his entire shift, nor did he see anyone carrying a large parcel or anyone acting suspiciously. Describing the layout of the station, Groves stated that someone entering from the street would have to pass the ticket collector to get to the ladies' lavatory but if they arrived by train, they could get to the lavatory and, indeed, back to the platform, without having to walk past the collector. Groves also confirmed that he had heard no screams or other unusual sounds that evening but pointed out that a child's cries from the waiting room would doubtless have been drowned by the roar and rattle of passing trains.

Four-year-old Alice Scott was carried into the inquest by her father but was completely overcome by shyness and refused to speak a word. At the coroner's suggestion, Betsy Scott was brought back into the witness box to put the questions to her daughter on his behalf but Alice was having none of it and simply buried her face in her mother's neck

Police surgeon Dr James Kearney confirmed that Maggie Nally had been violently sexually assaulted, either shortly before or immediately after her death, adding that he was of the opinion that she died at about 10.00 p.m. Having visited the station shortly after Maggie was found Kearney told the inquest that he was confident that the lavatory cubicle was the scene of the child's rape. It was then left for Dr Bernard Spilsbury to take the witness stand and give an account of his post-mortem examination.

'Dr Spilsbury is too eminent a medical man to make a mistake in his calculations...'

When Maggie Nally's body was discovered, the job of conducting a full post-mortem examination fell to celebrated Home Office pathologist Dr Bernard Spilsbury. An authoritative, handsome, charismatic and erudite man, Spilsbury first came to public prominence as an expert witness for the prosecution in the trial of American Hawley Harvey Crippen, who was convicted in 1910 of poisoning his wife in Holloway, London and was subsequently executed. Spilsbury's evidence on a so-called abdominal scar proved crucial in identifying the scant remains of Crippen's wife, which were found buried in the cellar of the home they had rented in Holloway and completely invalidated Crippen's defence that his wife had left him to go back to America with another man.

In 1925, Norman Thorne was convicted of the murder of his girlfriend. Thorne insisted that Elsie Cameron committed suicide and that he had panicked on finding her hanging from a beam in a barn on his chicken farm in Crowborough, Sussex, and disposed of her body. Although the evidence against Thorne was flimsy, such was Spilsbury's commanding presence in court and his unshakeable faith in the correctness of his own evidence that the jury were apparently swayed by his reputation and found Thorne guilty of murder. Awaiting his eventual execution at Wandsworth Prison, Thorne wrote to his father, describing himself as '... a martyr to Spilsburyism.'

Ten years before Thorne's trial, having examined the remains of Maggie Nally, Spilsbury concluded that the cause of the little girl's death was asphyxia due to the introduction of a foreign body into the mouth, followed by heart failure or syncope, which Spilsbury attributed to *status lymphaticus.* This suggests that, in the course of his examination, Spilsbury discovered that Maggie had what he believed to be an enlarged thymus gland and although Spilsbury's findings were consistent with the medical knowledge of the time, *status lymphaticus* is a condition that we now know does not exist.

In April 1914, exactly a year before Maggie's murder, a 'medical correspondent' writing in *The Manchester Guardian,* described the condition of *status lymphaticus* as '...bodily debility and a greatly reduced power of resistance, which makes its subjects – generally children but occasionally young adults – liable to death from such trivial causes as the prick of a pin, a sudden plunge into cold water, the administration of an anaesthetic or the occurrence of a mild infectious disease or a baby may be found dead in its cot without there having been any reason to anticipate its death'. Examination of contemporary newspapers at around the time of Maggie Nally's death reveals several deaths attributed to this condition, including that of eight-year-old Lily Bowers of Sale, Cheshire, whose sudden death while at school was attributed to *status lymphaticus* and heart failure, due to her having eaten a heavy lunch.

The thymus gland is an organ located directly beneath the breastbone in humans and forms part of our immune system, playing a major part in our ability to fight disease. However, until the 1930's, it was thought of as an 'organ of mystery', as doctors were unable to figure out its true function.

It was first suggested that the thymus might simply act as a protective cushion for other organs within the thoracic cavity or that it might be responsible for regulating lung function in babies and infants. In 1777, Hewson published the results of his study on the thymus, which was based on observations of dogs and calves (Jacobs et al, 1999). Hewson confirmed earlier theories that the size of the gland increases from birth to puberty and concluded that it was a type of lymph gland but almost sixty years later, Sir Astley Cooper published a contradictory paper, suggesting that the gland's only purpose was to fill the space in the thoracic cavity, which would eventually be taken up by an infant's lungs when they grew to maturity.

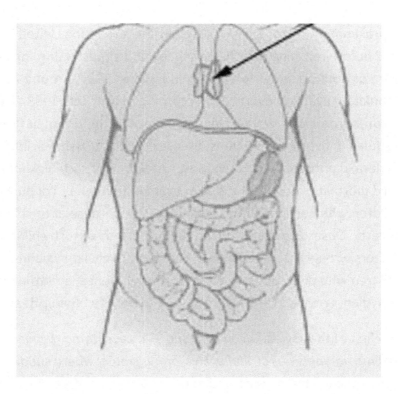

Diagram showing the position of the thymus gland

Until the 19ᵗʰ century, it was widely medically accepted that the human thymus gland served no real useful purpose. However, during the latter part of that century, there was an increased interest in child welfare issues and a particular concern for seemingly normal, healthy children who died suddenly and unexpectedly. Whereas such tragedies had previously been categorised as 'death by visitation of God', coroners now demanded a more scientific and precise medical explanation and, in 1874, the passing of a new Births and Deaths Registration Act made stating a cause of death compulsory (Dally, 1997.) This led to an increase in the number of post mortem examinations conducted on children and doctors quickly discovered that babies and children who died suddenly appeared to have disproportionately large thymus glands.

What nobody realised at the time was that illness and stress can shrink the size of the thymus gland by up to 75%. During the 1900's, approximately 140 of every 1000 children born in the United Kingdom died before reaching their first birthday and almost a third of all deaths were of children under five (Hicks and Allen, 1999) . Around 25% of the population lived in poverty and according to Mitchell (1988), half of the children from poor, working class families died before their fifth birthday, most from infectious diseases such as diarrhoea, influenza, cholera, diphtheria and tuberculosis. At a time of such high infant and child mortality, most post mortem examinations were conducted on children who had died either from illness or because of the effects of poverty. Observing the shrunken thymus glands of such children, doctors wrongly assumed that the comparatively large glands of children who died suddenly were abnormal. Hence, according to Hicks and Allen, two new terms were coined to denote 'thymic death'

The first of these was '*thymic asthma*', (a.k.a. *asthma thymicum, Kopp asthma, laryngismus stridulus* and *laryngismus*), where sudden death was explained by the obstruction or compression of a child's airway by an enlarged thymus gland, which physically prevented the child from breathing. Although the very existence of thymic asthma was being discounted by doctors as early as 1858, it persisted as an explanation for sudden infant deaths well into the 1920's.

Towards the end of the 19th century, the diagnosis of *thymic asthma* was increasingly replaced by one of *status lymphaticus* (a.k.a. *constitution-lymphatica, lymphatic constitution, lymphatic-chlorotic constitution, lymphatic diathesis, lymphatic dyscrasia, lymphatic habitus, lymphatism, status thymicolymphaticus, status thymicus* and *thymo-lympaticus*). Whereas *thymic asthma* involved compression or occlusion of a child's airway, s*tatus lymphaticus* suggested an abnormality of the entire lymphatic or immune system, characterised by enlarged thymus gland, tonsils, spleen and lymph nodes. Affected children tended to be '...well fed, pale, pasty, flabby and rather inert and effeminate, with large thymus and tonsils... but otherwise healthy' (Guntheroth, 1999). In 1898, Osler described what he called 'the lymphatic constitution', stating that sufferers had '...a diminished vital resistance and are especially prone to fatal collapse under ordinarily very inadequate exciting causes'. One of the purposes served by *status lymphaticus* was to provide an explanation for the sudden deaths of children while under anaesthetic, in order to prevent surgeons being held responsible.

The preoccupation with the enlarged thymus gland and the belief that those children with large glands were at grave risk from sudden death led to attempts being made either to shrink the thymus using radiology or to surgically remove it completely. In 1908, almost a third of all children whose thymus glands were removed died on the operating table (Jacobs et al, 1999), while many of those children treated with X-Rays went on to develop cancer.

It wasn't until 1931 that a report was published in *The Lancet* announcing 'The End of *Status Lymphaticus'*. A specially appointed committee from the Medical Research Council and Pathological Society of Great Britain and Ireland set out to establish a normal range for the thymus gland. The results obtained showed that the weight of the average thymus gland at birth was equivalent to fifteen grams, increasing to thirty-five grams at puberty then gradually declining in size, weighing less than five grams in old age. By examining records of cases of sudden death, researchers established that there was absolutely no evidence of *status lymphaticus* as a pathological entity and concluded '...we have to accept the fact that a few people, especially children, die when we cannot see why they should.'

Given that Maggie had supposedly been seen near a whelk stall and that she had also allegedly been given a dried fig by bus conductor Redman, Spilsbury paid particular attention to searching for remnants of these foods among her stomach contents. He found neither but did find remains of an apple, including pips. Since nobody could recall Maggie having eaten an apple that afternoon, the probability is that she either bought one herself with the money given to her by her aunt and grandfather or one was given to her by her killer. It must be remembered that although Spilsbury found no trace of fig or fig seeds in Maggie's digestive tract, Redman only stated that he gave her a fig – he did not see her put it into her mouth and in order for remnants to be found in her stomach it is obvious that Maggie had to have actually eaten it.

It was estimated that Maggie Nally died at around 10.00 p.m. and, having made a preliminary examination of the contents of her stomach, Spilsbury found '...remnants of meat, to which hair was attached'. Further analysis of Maggie's stomach contents led Spilsbury to the conclusion that she had eaten a meal of giblets and breast mutton within three hours of her death, most probably only ninety minutes before dying. Maggie was known to have eaten a lunch of breast mutton and giblets at home with her family at lunchtime on the day of her death but Spilsbury was adamant that, unless she suffered from severe indigestion, she had eaten a second identical meal shortly before she died.

Spilsbury described finding some small feathers, as well as meat from the neck of a fowl in Maggie's stomach, suggesting that the feathers indicated that the giblets had not been properly cleaned before they were cooked. Maggie's father gave weight to Spilsbury's theory of a second identical meal by insisting that the giblets his wife served at lunch had been thoroughly cleaned.

'Dr Spilsbury is too eminent a medical man to make a mistake in his calculations, so that the only conclusion they [the police] can come to is that by a strange coincidence the girl had a similar meal in a dwelling house outside her own home and naturally in the house of the stranger who attracted her away from the district' reported the newspapers of 18 April 1915. Although giblets and mutton were described as '...common enough on the tables of the poor', the police were adamant that it was extremely unlikely that such fare would be served in eating houses or even street stalls in the area, particularly on Easter Sunday. Maggie's parents were both out on the afternoon of 4 April and it was suggested that Maggie may have gone home in their absence and eaten some leftovers, before going out again. However, there were other occupants of the house present that afternoon and nobody saw her return, so this theory was discounted. Thus it was accepted that, although it might be a strange coincidence, someone had given Maggie a second identical meal to the lunch she ate with her parents.

Only police surgeon Dr James Kearney seemed in the least sceptical about Spilsbury's conclusions, expressing an opinion that it was highly unlikely that Maggie had eaten a second meal. Kearney believed that Maggie had probably bolted her food in her haste to go out and had then moved about quickly, causing her digestion to be retarded. It was likely that the meat she ate was fatty and, being meat, would be naturally high in protein, both of which would cause her lunch to be digested more slowly. Since we are now aware that fear, anxiety and distress can retard digestion, it seems probable that Maggie's last meal was eaten at her parents' home at lunchtime but, given Spilsbury's reputation at the time, his conclusions were accepted without question.

'He had the appearance of a respectable working man.'

From the very outset, it was almost inevitable that the murder of Maggie Nally would be compared to three other unsolved child murders of the period, those of six-year-old Marie Ellen Bailes which occurred on 29 May 1908, twelve-year-old Winifred Baker on 6 December 1912 and five-year-old Willie Starchfield on 8 January 1914.

On 30 May 1908 at around 8.45 a.m., a man struggled down the steps into a public lavatory at the end of St George's Road, Elephant and Castle, carefully carrying a large, heavy and seemingly quite fragile parcel, which was wrapped in brown paper and securely tied with thin rope. Twenty-eight-year-old William Joseph Votier [15] was cleaning the steps on his last ever day as a lavatory attendant when the man approached him and asked to have one of the toilet cubicle doors opened. The man seemed somewhat agitated and nervous as he placed the parcel at his feet in order to free his hands to find a 1d coin, which he handed to Votier, who opened the door and then carried on with his cleaning.

Elephant and Castle (author's collection)

Votier didn't see the man again and assumed that he had left the toilets by the alternative exit at the other end of the building. However, ten minutes later, when Votier went down the steps into the toilet area, he spotted that the man had left his parcel behind in the cubicle. Votier moved the package out into the corridor and stood contemplating it for a few minutes, wondering whether or not he should open it. He was joined by a colleague and, after a few more minutes of deliberation they came to the conclusion that the parcel could not have been left in the lavatory accidentally and tore away a small section of the paper, revealing a child's hand.

Sickened, the two attendants summoned a policeman and when PC George Aylward saw what they had uncovered, he immediately sent for the Divisional Police Surgeon of Scotland Yard, Dr George M. Henry. When Henry unwrapped the parcel, he found the naked body of a fair-haired little girl who was 'trussed up like a fowl.' Having removed three sheets of brown paper, each measuring 44 ½" x 29", Henry revealed a blanket measuring 7'2" x 5'6", which had a pattern of red, yellow and blue lines around the outside. Although clean, the blanket was darned and much worn, with a red binding that was completely missing at one end. Because of the way in which the blanket was creased, police believed that it had been used over a mattress on a bed. They agreed that it was taken from '...a tidy, thrifty and respectable domicile', most probably the killer's lodgings and appealed to all landladies and lodging-house keepers to check their rooms for missing blankets.

The little girl's throat had been cut horizontally from left to right for 3¾", severing all of the major blood vessels and she also had a deep cut on her chest that was 15½" long. Around her waist was a rope similar to a clothes line tied with a running knot, which had been used to pull her legs up, so that her thighs rested on her abdomen and her lower legs rested on the back of her thighs. The neck and chin were wrapped in strips of calico and flannelette, which were apparently torn from a child's pinafore and chemise. Henry estimated that the little girl had been dead for between twelve and fifteen hours and noted the presence of a great deal of loose, dry, sandy earth in her mouth, nose, eyes and in her wounds, which he believed indicated that she had either been buried or at least covered with earth or that she had been placed on a sanded floor, such as that found in a livery stable, public house or even a garden path. There was also a bruise behind the child's right ear [16] and Henry concluded that she may have been hit on the head and stunned before her throat was cut. There had been no attempt to rape or otherwise sexually assault the victim and the cause of death was shock loss of blood from the wound in her throat, which Henry believed had been inflicted by somebody standing behind or to the right of the child. The surgeon thought that the cut to the chest was probably inflicted after death and could have been the beginnings of an abandoned attempt at dissecting the body.

Meanwhile, after his six-year-old daughter failed to return home from school on the afternoon of 29 May, gutta percha worker Alfred Henry Bailes spent a long and anxious night cycling around London, calling at hospitals and police stations. Marie Ellen Bailes and her nine-year-old brother Alfred junior came home from school for lunch, setting off at 1.40 p.m. to return to St John's Roman Catholic School in Duncan Terrace, Islington. (It should be remembered that police investigating Maggie's murder were contacted by a family from Duncan Terrace to say that their daughter had been enticed away by a man while on an errand to buy a newspaper but fortunately she had managed to evade him and run home.)

Marie's father described his daughter as being in the very best of spirits when she left the house, adding that he gave her a penny just before she went, which she was known to have later spent on sweets. Golden-blonde haired, blue eyed Marie was large for her age and at 3' 10", was almost as tall as her older brother. When last seen she was wearing a blue cotton dress, a white pinafore with a frill at the neck, black cotton stockings, button boots, a black velvet 'skullcap' with a rosette at each side, a new white flannelette petticoat, a pink flannelette petticoat, white drawers, a white flannelette chemise and a red and grey tartan under vest [17]. She carried a check schoolbag and wore a small Roman Catholic medal bearing the image of the Virgin Mary around her neck on a piece of blue silk ribbon.

When school finished, Alfred junior was half an hour late leaving and did not see his sister, assuming that she had left with one of her friends, as she often did. When Marie didn't arrive home from school, her worried parents first contacted her playmates and when nobody could enlighten them as to their daughter's whereabouts, they reported her missing to the local police, before her father began his night-long search, scouring the streets of London for any trace of little Marie. Mrs Bailes was confident that her daughter, who was very shy, would not speak to a strange man or woman in the street, having been told that if she was ever approached, she was to run away at once.

As a missing child, Marie's description was circulated to all police stations in London and when the body was found in the lavatory, Detective Inspector Ferret communicated with the police at Islington, who took Mr Bailes to the mortuary at Southwark. Bailes took one look at the body and exclaimed 'Yes, yes, that's her' before collapsing.

An inquest was opened on 2 June by Francis Danford Thomas, the Deputy Coroner for Southwark. Although Marie's mother Mary Agnes Bailes was present, she was almost prostrate with grief and so it was left to her husband to confirm his daughter's identity and relate what was known of her last movements. Bailes was able to positively identify the strips of calico and flannelette that had been wrapped around the child's face and neck as having been torn from Marie's undergarments, however neither he nor his wife recognised the blanket in which the body was wrapped.

One of the chief witnesses at the inquest was eleven-year-old Thomas Bone, who went to the same school as Marie and also lived near her and who claimed to have seen Marie walking home with a girl named Maria Kirsch (or Kersch). He spoke to Marie, asking her where she was going and she replied 'I am going home'. Bone then told her that her brother was coming and, knowing that this meant that she was late, Marie instantly broke into a run. According to Bone she was then only a few houses away from her home. The police spoke to Maria, who was only six years old and she vehemently denied walking home with Marie after school on 29 May. 'Then that negatives all this witnesses evidence' (sic) complained the coroner, who then asked for Bone to be recalled. Under further questioning, Bone refused to be swayed from his assertion that Maria Kirsch walked home from school with Marie on the afternoon of her disappearance.

Police surgeon Henry described Marie's injuries and informed the coroner that the child had eaten a heavy meal consisting of meat and potatoes shortly before her death.

The lavatory attendant was called and told the inquest about finding the parcel with its gruesome contents. He described the man who left it as '...a fairly well-spoken fellow', aged about thirty-three years old, 5' 6 or 7" tall, with a fair complexion, light brown hair and a light brown moustache. The man was of thin build and was wearing a dark tweed suit or jacket and waistcoat with grey trousers, a double linen collar, a dark tweed cap and a black 'sailor' tie. 'He had the appearance of a respectable working man' concluded Votier [18].

As the coroner prepared to adjourn the inquest, a member of the public tried to interject and question the medical evidence. Quashed by the coroner, Alexander MacDonald then attempted to address the jury and was ejected from the proceedings.

Newspapers reported that more than a thousand police officers were involved in trying to apprehend the murderer and in the course of their investigations they quickly identified some key suspects. They were told of a man who was hanging around Prebend Street, Islington, where Marie lived with her family, speaking to young girls. The man was described as '...not very tall, brown hair, wearing dark clothes, a cloth check cap – probably tweed – and a black and white tie.' Another man, said to have a noticeable lump on his neck, was alleged to have loitered near Marie's school, where he pulled faces at young girls and generally behaved in a strange manner. The police arrested a suspect who closely matched the description of the man who abandoned the parcel in the lavatory. Painter Llewellyn Denbigh of Marlborough Road was apprehended in Derby, having travelled there from London on the morning of 30 May. However, it was quickly evident that Denbigh had nothing to do with Marie's murder and he was released from custody without charge.

On 8 June, an inmate of Wandsworth Work House, who closely matched the description of the wanted man, was brought to the attention of the police when it was noticed that his clothes were blood stained. However, having been interviewed by officers from Scotland Yard, he was quickly eliminated from the police enquiries and released without charge. Police were aware that a lunatic, who was classed as a homicidal maniac, had recently escaped from Bexley Heath Asylum, where he was normally confined to the dangerous ward. When he made his escape, Thomas Bradley, who had a sallow complexion and dark brown hair, was said to have been wearing a dark tweed suit, such as that remembered by lavatory attendant. However, Bradley eventually handed himself in to the police roughly two weeks after the murder and was ruled out as a suspect.

A stationer from Barnet claimed to have sold stiff brown paper to a man matching the description given by Votier. The man told the female assistant that he needed the paper for '...wrapping garments and such like articles' and, having been shown a selection, he bought three penny worth. However, within days, a police spokesman commented 'It is remarkable how many shopkeepers in and near London sold brown paper and string on Friday to a man matching the description issued by Scotland Yard'. The police found no traces of unexplained fingerprints, either on the paper or on the body itself.

It was noted that the lavatory in which the body was dumped was close to the station of the City and South London Electric Tube Railway, which was directly linked to the Angel of Islington Station. Police theorised that Marie's killer had transported her body from Islington to Elephant and Castle by tube train. The police interviewed all railway workers on the Bakerloo line, including a guard named Mr Holland, who claimed to have seen a man matching the lavatory attendant's description and carrying a brown paper parcel making such a journey on the morning of 30 May. A publican and a barman both saw a man carrying a parcel in a public house near Elephant and Castle at around 6.45 a.m. on the morning of 30 May and stated that the man placed the parcel on the floor while he drank a glass of whisky. All three witnesses were confident that they would recognise the man if they ever saw him again.

In spite of reports in the newspapers to the contrary, the police did not find Marie's clothes, although they did find a bundle of man's clothing close to a river, the banks of which had very sandy soil. It was suggested that the man who killed Marie might have then committed suicide by drowning but the investigating officers found no evidence to support that claim, nor did they give any credence to a theory that the cruciform arrangement of Marie's wounds suggested that her murder was the work of a religious maniac. A child's small gilt crucifix was found in Kensington Park but Marie was known to have been wearing a small, oval religious medal when she disappeared, rather than a cross[19].

Marie was buried on 6 June 1908, when a crowd of around ten thousand people lined the streets, many following the hearse all the way from Prebend Street to St Mary's Roman Catholic Cemetery, Kensal Green. By that time, the police were no closer to discovering the identity of her killer and, although several arrests had been made, all of the suspects were eventually released without charge. The coroner re-opened the inquest on 16 June and almost immediately adjourned it again for a further two weeks. When the proceedings finally concluded on 2 July, it was not without another outburst from Alexander

MacDonald, who wished to inform the jury of his belief that the crime had been committed by a woman. The coroner asked if the police had considered this theory and were told that it had been discounted.

The police informed the coroner that their enquiries thus far had brought no good result and the inquest jury found that 'Death occurred from shock due to haemorrhage through severance of the vessels of the throat and neck, committed by some person or persons unknown'. They returned a formal verdict that Marie Ellen Bailes was wilfully murdered by some person or persons unknown.

In June 1909, a five-year-old girl was stabbed more than twenty times at Edgware. Frederick Burgess confessed to the murder and was later tried, found insane and sentenced to be detained during His Majesty's Pleasure. Police established that Burgess had been in prison at the time of Marie's murder and therefore could not have been her killer.

On 17 August 1912, eight-year-old Harold Payne was found in Peckham Rye Park with his throat cut. All Harold was able to say was that 'someone did it'. Harold survived the assault, as did a second victim of the same attacker, draper's assistant Ethel Clarke who was seized from behind on 22 August and her throat slashed with a table knife. The attack on Ethel Clarke was witnessed by Walter D. Thomson, who surreptitiously followed the attacker until he spotted a policeman and then quietly drew the constable's attention to what he had just seen. Twenty-five-year-old George Clay was taken to Brixton Prison to await his trial, where the medical officer Sidney Reginald Dyer described him as '...a chronic epileptic; he has had fits ever since his early youth, sometimes as many as three or four a week. He was very excited and at times incoherent, agitated and emotional... His family history shows that several relatives on his father's side suffered from epileptic insanity, and he himself on one occasion attempted suicide by taking carbolic acid. I consider that he is now insane, and that at the time of committing this offence he was insane and not responsible for his act. He is a very dangerous lunatic.'

At his trial at the Old Bailey, Clay was found guilty but insane and sentenced to be detained during His Majesty's pleasure. Although he was at liberty at the time of Marie's murder and his throat-slashing method was similar to that used by her killer, the act of wrapping her body in brown paper and disposing of it in a public lavatory seems too sophisticated for a perpetrator such as Clay. It is thought that he was sent to Broadmoor Criminal Lunatic Asylum, where he is believed to have died in 1918.

15. In the newspaper accounts of the crime, the lavatory attendant is given a variety of different names. These include William Joseph Votier, Joseph Voter, James Voter, Joseph Potren and Mr Goosetrey. Since records show that there was a William Joseph Votier working as a Borough Council Attendant at the time, I have elected to use that name.

16. Some newspapers state that the site of the blow was behind Marie's left ear.

17. Some reports described the under vest as being black and white check.

18. Apart from his dark jacket and tweed cap, the description of the man's physical features bears little resemblance to the one given to the officers investigating Maggie's murder by the family from Duncan Terrace, who described the man that attempted to abduct their daughter as being of medium height, clean shaven, with very fresh complexion and dark hair. There were however some similarities with the description of the soldier supposedly seen with Maggie, who was described by the bus conductor as about thirty years old and 5' 8 or 9" tall. He looked ill and had a very sallow complexion, brown hair, a short light brown moustache and around three days' growth of whiskers on a 'medium face'.

19. Some newspapers report that the trinket found in Kensington Park was not a crucifix but a religious medal identical to Marie's. However, as the papers pointed out, such medals were worn by thousands of children and there was nothing to connect the one found with the murdered child.

'Your temperance teacher wants to see you'.

The murder of Maggie Nally was also compared to that of twelve-year-old Winifred 'Winnie' Beatrice Baker, which took place in 1912. Although Winnie's murder was in Woking not London and there was no obvious connection with the railway, those who believed that her killer went on to murder Maggie three years later argued that there were very good rail links between the town and the capital.

On the evening of 5 December 1912, Winnie went to a regular meeting of the Nightingale Scouts at the Mission Hall in Walton Road, Woking and unusually, she attended the meeting without her identical twin sister, Enid. At around 7.00 p.m. she left the hall with two friends, Doris Soper and Olive Simmonds. All three girls were carrying scout poles and Winnie was also holding a piece of paper, on which was printed pictures of flags.

The girls stopped to buy some sweets from a shop, when a man suddenly walked up behind Doris and tapped her on the shoulder.

'Your temperance teacher wants to see you' he told her.

'We are not Band of Hope Girls, we are Nightingales' Doris protested.

'That's right' the man agreed, asking Doris to go with him.

Doris and Olive refused but Winnie told them 'I will go and see what she wants. You wait here, I won't be a minute'. Her friends were not about to let her go off alone with a strange man and, rather than waiting, they followed after her but when the man realised they were there, he pulled Winnie along faster and they lost sight of her near the Mission Hall. Having spoken to the caretaker, who hadn't seen either Winnie or her companion, Doris and Olive went straight off to find a policeman to tell him what had happened.

Although search parties were quickly organised and people began looking for Winnie almost immediately, it wasn't until 7.00 a.m. the next day that her body was found in a passage near the Mission Hall. Since the area around the hall had already been thoroughly searched during the night, it was assumed that her abductor had taken her to a nearby common or an empty house and killed her there, dumping her body later.

Dr Bertram Howill (or Howell) examined Winnie where she lay on her back on the path, her feet facing towards a gate. Her scarf had been wrapped tightly around her neck twice and tied at the front with a single knot and Howill was able to determine that the cause of death was strangulation. He estimated that Winnie had been dead for at least six hours and confirmed that she had been 'outraged'. He also noted that her brown velvet jacket was muddy and that her boots were not laced, from which he concluded that they had been removed and then later replaced on her feet.

Olive Simmonds (left) and Doris Soper (right), 1912. Inset Winnie Baker.

Author's collection

Both Olive and Doris were sure that they had seen the man who went off with Winnie before, only a couple of days earlier on 3 December, as they returned from another scouts' meeting. At that time he was wearing a black overcoat with a cap and a white muffler - he was with another man and didn't speak to them as he passed. After seeing him for a second time on 5 December, they described him as: 'Aged around twenty-five, medium height, with a ginger moustache. Full faced, dressed in a brown suit with stripes, wearing a trilby or similar shaped hat and a light coloured overcoat. Has the appearance of a mechanic.' When he walked off with Winnie, her friends told the investigating officers that the man appeared to know her and addressed her by her name. They also told the police that the man had a pronounced stutter and a habit of holding his hand in front of his mouth when he spoke.

When her body was found, Winnie's hat, scout pole and picture of flags were missing, although her hat was subsequently found a short distance away from her body and handed in to the police.

Acting coroner Mr E. H. White opened an inquest on Winnie's death on 9 December. After evidence of identification was given by her father, William Thomas Baker, the inquest heard from Frederick William Church, who found Winnie's body and Ernest John Girton, who found her brown felt hat lying in the street. When Dr Howill had given his evidence, White adjourned the inquest to allow the police more time to investigate.

The police firmly believed that Winnie's killer was a local man, since he apparently knew his victim by name and was aware that the Mission Hall was used for both Nightingale Scouts and Band of Hope meetings. A suggestion that the murderer had fled to Exeter by train was followed up but the trail went cold. Police complained that the description of the suspect was so vague that it might fit scores of individuals and appealed for the man's companion on 3 December to contact them.

There was a brief flurry of excitement when a man shot himself in Woking only a couple of days after the murder. However, police quickly concluded that the suicide of sixty-year-old Thomas James Harris Read had absolutely no connection to Winnie's death.

When the inquest concluded, the police had been unable to apprehend Winnie's killer and the jury returned a verdict of 'wilful murder by person or persons unknown.' Her murder remains unsolved.

'No conscientious jury would hang a cat on evidence of that kind.'

In January 1914, five-year-old William Starchfield, affectionately known as Willie, lived with his mother Agnes in lodgings at 191 Hampstead Road, Camden. His parents were separated, either because of his father John's ill-treatment of his wife and child or because of arguments between his parents about money, depending on which newspaper report is believed.

Tottenham Court Road (author's collection). The Horse Shoe Hotel is on the right of the picture (with canopy onto pavement). Note the news stand, bottom left of the picture.

John Starchfield lived in a lodging house off Long Acre, near The Strand, and sold newspapers for a living. On 27 September 1912, the former soldier became a minor local celebrity when a murder occurred at The Horse Shoe Hotel, at the end of Tottenham Court Road, near where he had his paper stall. Having shot and killed barmaid Esther May Towers and wounded several other people (one of whom later died from his injuries), twenty-eight-year-old Armenian Stephen Titus ran from the premises, still wildly firing his gun. Although unarmed, Starchfield bravely tackled the gunman and was shot in the stomach for his trouble. However due to this intervention, Titus was apprehended and, when Starchfield came out of hospital, he was awarded £50 for his bravery, along with an allowance of £1 a week from the Carnegie Hero Fund, which he handed over to his wife each week as maintenance for their son. Yet Agnes still struggled to make ends meet and on 8 January 1914, with only a single penny left in her pocket, she went out to look for tailoring work, leaving her son in the care of her landlady, Sarah Longstaff. Before leaving, Agnes sent her son out to fetch a loaf of bread and, when he returned at 12.15 p.m., she gave Mrs Longstaff permission to send Willie to run errands for her, if she had any that needed doing.

Sarah Longstaff took Agnes at her word and at 12.30 p.m., she sent Willie to a nearby stationers shop to buy some 'Apartments to Let' cards to place in her window. Willie returned with the cards fifteen minutes later but they were not what Mrs Longstaff wanted and he was sent back to get replacements. Willie left his lodgings at 1.00 p.m. and at 4.30 p.m., his body was found stuffed under a seat of a third-class train carriage on the North London Railway, running between Chalk Farm to Broad Street. He had been strangled.

The stationer's shop to which Willie was sent was only twenty-two houses along the road from his lodgings in Hampstead Street and Mr Knapp the shop manager clearly remembered Willie coming in for the second time and exchanging the cards. The police initially concentrated their enquiries in the area around the child's home and the stationery shop and spoke to a six-year-old Italian boy named Angelo Portinari, who was a playmate of Willie's. Although he spoke almost no English, Angelo gave a statement, which was translated by his older brother. He told the police that he had seen Willie at about 1.00 p.m., when he was with an older boy who was slightly taller than Willie and was wearing a dark suit and a peaked cap. (Angelo particularly remembered the day of his playmate's disappearance because he was taken to the cinema later that afternoon.) According to Angelo, Willie was walking towards Camden Town, carrying a bundle of firewood and, as he passed the Portinari family's coffee shop, he dropped one of the sticks. When he bent to pick it up, his companion urged him to 'Come along'. Willie was known to have come home very late more than once before and, on the last occasion, had told his worried mother that 'a big boy' had taken him to the cinema. However, as far as Agnes Starchfield was aware, the 'big boy' that her son was referring to was a local boy named Speller, who was only eight or nine years old and so hardly likely to be a threat to Willie's safety.

Willie was a distinctive looking child, having a mop of fair, curly hair, which he wore in shoulder length ringlets, dark eyes and a rather pale face. On the day of his disappearance, he was dressed in a blue serge knickerbocker suit and a soft cloth hat, with no collar and tie, along with brown stockings and brown boots which reached above his ankle. As soon as his description was published, a bus driver, John Nixon, and his conductor, Mr Cudd, came forward to inform police that they believed that Willie had been riding on their bus at about 3.30 p.m. on 8 January, travelling between Kentish Town Railway Station and Tufnell Park Tube Station. Both men visited the mortuary to view Willie's body and remained positive that they were correct in their identification. They told the police that the boy was accompanied by a 'foreign-looking man', with long delicate fingers, who dragged the boy almost brutally onto the bus and pushed him upstairs to sit on the open top deck, in spite of the fact that it was cold and raining at the time.

The police were sceptical about this supposed sighting since the medical evidence suggested that Willie was dead before 3.30 p.m. and there was no direct route from Tufnell Park Tube Station to any station on the North London Railway. When a cord noose with some long brown hair attached to it was found on the staircase at Tufnell Park Tube Station, the police decided that it was not connected to the murder. In the early stages of the investigation, they were inundated with what they described as 'vague clues', including a multitude of bits of string and tape picked up at various places. People were keen to share '...suggestions, theories, identifications and innuendoes' - numerous members of the public claimed to have experienced visions or dreams about the crime and one psychic even supplied the police with a drawing of the face of the murderer.

Hampstead Road, 1907 (author's collection)

The police revealed that Willie Starchfield had apparently been seen in almost every part of London at the crucial times, except for the area around Hampstead Road, from where he vanished. Investigators could scarcely believe that nobody had seen the boy and an in an effort to jog peoples' memories, they stressed the uniqueness of his hair, telling the newspapers 'An ordinary child might have passed unobserved, perhaps, but Willie with his long curls, was a boy who usually attracted notice'. After receiving the preliminary post-mortem results, police appealed to the public for anyone who either gave or sold cake to Willie to come forward, since the analysis of his stomach contents suggested that he had eaten something containing currants, sultanas, raisins and coconut – most probably a piece of cake - within two or three hours of his death. Willie had earlier eaten a breakfast of bread pudding that contained spices and dried fruit but, according to his mother, no coconut.

House-to-house enquiries were conducted in Hampstead Road and the police urged homeowners to search their gardens for the missing 'Apartment to Let' cards that Willie was known to have collected from the shop before his disappearance. In a quest to find them, police appealed to road sweepers to cast their minds back to 8 January to see if they could recall sweeping up any such cards. They also interviewed every bus driver, tram driver and conductor, whose route took him through Hampstead Road and spoke to all personnel at every one of the stations on the North London Railway. A police spokesman reassured the public that 'All the known facts are being weighed and re-weighed, all possible theories tested and all the sources of information whence some light might be thrown on the crime are being tried'.

A conductor on the Charing Cross Tube Railway came forward to say that he had seen a man carrying a child at Goodge Street Tube Station, who caught either the 1.18 or the 2.02 p.m. train travelling north, disembarking at Camden Town Station at either 1.24 or 2.08 p.m. Mr Durdle recalled that the man was 5' 9 or 10" tall, between forty and forty-five years old, with high cheekbones, who was wearing a dirty grey tweed suit and a grey tweed cap. Durdle formed the impression that the man was either Irish or Italian, most probably the former since the man's dark, heavy moustache was clipped short and not worn in what he described as 'the Italian fashion'.

The man ran onto the platform to catch the train, with the child slung over his right shoulder. Durdle said that it struck him at the time that this was an unusual way to carry a child but thought nothing more of what he had seen until he read the reports of the murder.

Willie was described as a mother's boy, who was shy and mistrustful around strangers and thus his mother was confident that he would have strongly resisted any attempt to take him anywhere, leading the investigating officers to the assumption that he probably went off with somebody that he knew. Since he was far too young to get onto the North London Railway on his own, it stood to reason that someone was with him and the police believed that the boy and his killer boarded the train at either Chalk Farm or Camden Town stations, passing through Maiden Lane, Caledonian Road, Highbury, Canonbury, Mildmay Park, Dalston and Haggerston (some of these stations have since closed). Nobody could determine whether Willie was actually strangled in the carriage where he was discovered or if he was killed elsewhere and his body then carried onto the train and dumped. If the former, then the murderer was likely to be undisturbed, since the carriage had no corridor and therefore no direct connection to other parts of the train. Yet he or she would have needed to work very quickly, since the longest run between stations was only three minutes. If the latter, the killer would have had to carry the child's dead body through the station and onto the train.

Coroner Dr William Wynn Westcott, by kind permission of Tim Stygall.

The inquest on Willie's death was opened at the Shoreditch Coroner's Court by coroner Dr William Wynn Westcott and promptly adjourned to allow the police more time to investigate the case. When it reopened on 22 January 1914, there was startling new evidence.

Signalman Joseph Rogers, who worked the signal box located at New Inn Yard, between Shoreditch and Broad Street, produced a looped section of blind cord that he had picked up from the line on the afternoon after the murder, which police surgeon Dr Garrett agreed could be the murder weapon. Garrett had initially examined the body within minutes of its discovery. At that time, the body was almost cold and the surgeon formed an opinion that death occurred between 2.00 and 3.00 p.m. on the afternoon of 8 January. Garrett determined that Willie was strangled with a '...narrow, constricting band', which had been applied with sufficient force to leave a distinct groove in the boy's neck. Garrett believed that Willie was either kneeling or lying down when he was murdered, as there were bruises on his torso consistent with his killer either kneeling on him or grasping him between their knees. His teeth were also loosened, as though pressure had been applied to his mouth. Scratch marks on Willie's throat and chest were indicative that the child fought to remove the noose from around his neck. However, pathologist Dr Bernard Spilsbury had also been asked to examine Willie's body and diagnosed *status lymphaticus,* which

'...gave rise to the danger of sudden death as the result of certain shocks and the lad would die more easily than a healthy boy.'

In contrast to the evidence of Garrett, who highlighted 'many superficial scratches and marks around the neck' as evidence of the child's attempts to prevent the constriction of the noose, Spilsbury told the inquest that Willie would probably have died within seconds of the application of the ligature. Both doctors did agree that 'there was no evidence of vice'.

The inquest then heard from two railway workers who separately claimed to have seen Willie with a man in the train as it passed them. Signalman George Robert Jackson testified that because of the child's long blond curls, he thought at first that Willie was a little girl. Having been to see Willie's body at the mortuary, he was certain that he had seen a man with a dark moustache, who was older than twenty-five and wearing a dark coat, get up from his seat and walk across the carriage to where Willie was sitting. Asked if he thought he would recognise the man again, Jackson said that he wouldn't.

Although he didn't actually see Willie, engine driver William Morcher told the inquest that he had seen a broad-shouldered, powerfully built man, wearing a dark overcoat in the carriage where the child's body was found.

The next witness at the inquest was Mrs Clara Frances Wood, whose evidence was to change the course of the entire police investigation. Mrs Wood recalled seeing a small boy with a mop of thick, light brown, curly hair walking hand in hand with a man, who she described as being thirty to forty years old, 5' 2 or 3" tall, with a dark complexion, dark hair and a dark moustache. When the jersey that Willie was wearing when he was murdered was produced in court, Mrs Wood claimed to recognise it and she also said that the boy had been eating a huge piece of cake, so big that he could barely hold it in his hand. Asked if she would recognise the man again, Mrs Wood dramatically pointed to Willie's father, John Starchfield.

'It's him' she stated.

John Starchfield had already told police that on the day of his son's murder, his gunshot wound was troubling him and so he stayed in bed until 3.30 p.m., at which time he went to his newspaper stand, where he remained until 7.00 p.m., before returning to his lodgings in pain and going straight back to bed. Since Mrs Wood was adamant that she had seen Starchfield with his son at 1.15 p.m. the coroner adjourned the inquest once again, to allow the police more time to investigate her testimony.

When the proceedings resumed a week later, another witness had come forward to say that he had seen a boy walking along Kentish Town Road to Camden Town Station with a man. Commercial traveller Richard John Wright described the man as about forty years old, 5' 4 or

5" tall, with a dark complexion and a heavy moustache. The man had broad shoulders and was wearing a dark overcoat and a dark Trilby hat. Although Wright recalled that the boy was about 3' 6" tall, slightly built and wearing tight clothing, he claimed not to have noticed the child's one outstanding distinguishing feature – his hair. When asked to identify the man he saw, Wright pointed to John Starchfield and when Starchfield spoke out to protest, Wright also claimed to recognise his voice, even though he had only actually heard the man speak three words, 'Come you here'.

The inquest jury returned a verdict of wilful murder against John Starchfield and he was swiftly arrested, still protesting his innocence. There followed a hearing before magistrates at the Old Street Police Court, during which ten witnesses were called who were able to give Starchfield an alibi, while still more witnesses claimed to have seen Willie with other people. John Reuben Symons saw the child with a woman aged between thirty-five and forty, and around 5' 2" tall. Symons recognised Willie by his distinctive hair and also said that he had noticed the child before, playing in the front garden of his home at 191 Hampstead Road.

Police located a woman and a boy of a similar age and appearance to Willie, who had been walking along Kentish Town Road at the time Symons claimed to have seen the victim. She was summoned to court by the prosecution and asked to walk towards Symons, holding her child's hand. However, Symons would not be swayed and stressed that neither the woman nor her son bore any resemblance to the woman and child he had seen, who he remained positive was Willie Starchfield.

Bus conductor Frederick Thomas Barnes was convinced that Willie and a woman rode his bus on 8 January. Barnes described the woman as twenty-five, with a pale complexion. His driver John Markham also remembered the woman and child, although he thought she was around thirty-five years old and was wearing dark clothing. Markham took particular notice of the couple, as his only son had died three years earlier and, like Willie, Markham's boy had a mop of blond ringlets.

One witness, John Moore, claimed to have seen Starchfield actually committing the murder. However, since he originally went to a magazine rather than to the police, his testimony was discredited, particularly after staff at the magazine offices related that Moore was drunk at the time and revealed that he had demanded payment for his information. (Between the magistrates' hearing and the trial, Moore unsuccessfully attempted suicide.)

In spite of the flimsiness of the evidence against him, Starchfield was committed for trial at the next Assizes. The proceedings opened on 31 March at the Old Bailey before Mr Justice Atkin but, having heard the case for the prosecution, Atkin dramatically halted the trial and ordered the jury to return a verdict of not guilty. According to the judge, the prosecution's entire case was based on evidence of identification and the witnesses couldn't even agree on that. Atkin also strongly criticised the inquest, calling it '...an entire mockery and a complete abuse of the duties entrusted to any coroner.' In an editorial of 2 April 1914, *The Manchester Guardian* commented 'No conscientious jury would hang a cat on evidence of that kind; the Crown, if it had not been compelled by the verdict of the coroner's jury, would never have thought of prosecuting it.'

John Starchfield was released from custody and died from consumption in April 1916, in the St Pancras Workhouse Infirmary. In June 1914, Agnes Starchfield was charged at Marylebone Police Court with threatening to commit suicide, after being found wandering the streets in her nightdress with a bottle of spirits of salts (hydrochloric acid) in her pocket. Agnes had given birth to three children, two of whom had died, leaving Willie as the only one to have survived beyond infancy and she had taken his loss very badly. Hearing this, the court took a sympathetic and lenient view of what was still at the time a criminal offence. She was handed over to her brother, who promised to take care of her.

In September 1916, a homeless man, John Fitzpatrick, handed himself in to the police and confessed to Willie's murder. Police found nothing to connect him with the crime and the murder of Willie Starchfield remains unsolved.

'...there were plenty of people about but no one took any notice.'

There are undoubtedly many similarities between the murders of Maggie Nally, Marie Bailes and Willie Starchfield, although the murder of Winnie Baker doesn't seem to quite fit the pattern of the other three, mainly because it took place in Woking rather than London. Additionally Winnie was considerably older than the other victims and was blatantly abducted in front of witnesses. Even so, at the time many people believed that the same hand was responsible for all four deaths.

Maggie, Marie and Willie were all around the same age and, although Willie was a boy, his long, blond curls gave him a feminine appearance and, at a distance, he was frequently mistaken for a girl. All of the three younger victims were said to be 'physically attractive' and big for their age and the fact that all are buried at Kensal Green Roman Catholic Cemetery suggests that they were all brought up in the Catholic faith (Marie and Maggie both went to Catholic schools). It would have been interesting to know if the police ever checked to see whether they shared any common acquaintances - for example, did they ever attend the same church or social events?

All four of the victims disappeared from an area with which they were familiar and one in which they would undoubtedly have felt safe and secure. Maggie was last seen only yards from her grandfather's and aunts' houses, while Marie was said to be just a few doors from home when she vanished, although the witness who saw her there was only eleven years old and, at the inquest, some doubt was cast on the accuracy of his evidence. Even so, Marie was apparently taken while on her regular route home from school. Willie was sent on an errand to a shop only twenty-two houses down the street from his lodgings and Winnie was walking home from a place where she attended meetings three times every week. Although the mothers of the three youngest victims all firmly believed that their child would not have gone off with a stranger, research conducted in recent years suggests that, even if warned about so-called stranger danger, most children of that age will quite happily go with someone they don't know (Furedi, 2008). That said, the three youngest children were all described as being unusually shy and mistrustful of strangers and statistically most child murders are committed by someone known to the victim, even if only as a casual acquaintance.

Looking at a present day map of London, it is also immediately obvious that all three of the younger victims were abducted in close proximity to what is now the A501 road, which runs from Paddington to the London Wall. Marie was taken in Islington, from a location somewhere between her school in Duncan Terrace and her home in Prebend Street. Duncan Terrace is very close to City Road, which forms part of the A501. Willie Starchfield was taken from Hampstead Road, which leads into Euston Road, another section of the A501, whereas Maggie Nally disappeared from the Edgware Road area, which adjoins the Marylebone Road part of the A501. The approximate distance between the three abduction points by road is around 4. 3 miles - less than 3 miles as the crow flies.

Maggie, Marie and Willie had all eaten food shortly before their deaths, which was believed to have been given to them by their abductors. Analysis of Willie's stomach contents suggested that he had eaten cake containing dried fruits and coconut, Marie had eaten a heavy meal of meat and potatoes, whereas Maggie was thought to have eaten another serving of stewed mutton and giblets. Even if the presence of this so-called second meal was explained by the slow digestion of her lunch, the unexplained remains of an apple were found in her stomach. Both Maggie and Willie were examined post-mortem by Dr Bernard Spilsbury and diagnosed with the condition *status lymphaticus*.

If the accounts of sightings given by the omnibus drivers and conductors are to be believed, both Maggie and Willie were transported on buses and both were taken to sit on the top deck, in the open air. Both were also reportedly spoken to quite roughly by the men they were with.

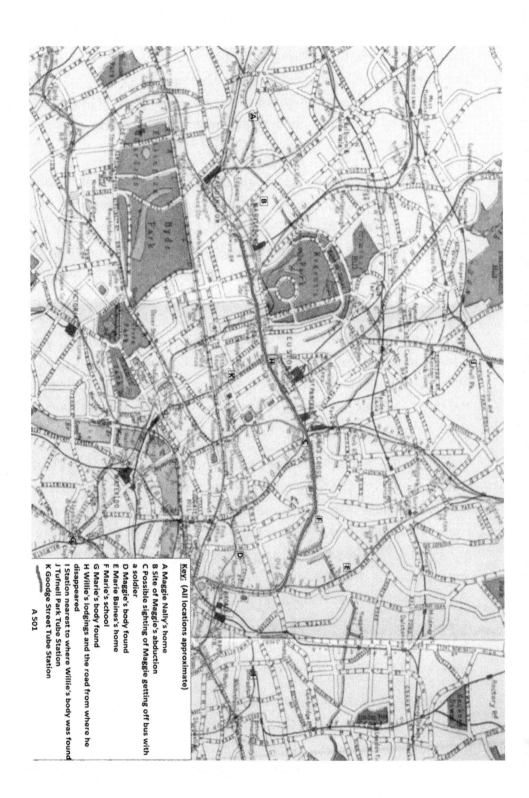

Key: (All locations approximate)

A Maggie Nally's home
B Site of Maggie's abduction
C Possible sighting of Maggie getting off bus with a soldier
D Maggie's body found
E Marie Baines's home
F Marie's school
G Marie's body found
H Willie's lodgings and the road from where he disappeared
I Station nearest to where Willie's body was found
J Tufnell Park Tube Station
K Goodge Street Tube Station

——— A 501

The circumstances of the deaths of the three youngest children suggest that each was killed by someone with an intimate working knowledge of London's railways and underground railways. The distance between the place where Marie was abducted and the location of the lavatory where she was found makes it almost certain that her killer used some kind of transport and the likelihood is that it was the tube. Either Willie's killer was able to despatch his victim and hide the body in the short time between stations, believed to have been a maximum of three minutes, or alternatively, the murderer was sufficiently confident to catch a train while carrying a child's body, which was then dumped under the seat. Maggie's killer either took the same risk of moving her dead body through a public area or was aware that the ladies' lavatory attendant would have gone off duty and felt certain that he wouldn't be disturbed as he raped and killed her. While Maggie's killer relied on a rag taken from her pocket to use as a murder weapon and Winnie was strangled with her own scarf, the fact that Willie was apparently strangled with a cord suggests that his killer probably went out equipped to kill, making his a premeditated rather than an opportunistic murder, with Willie either a specific target or a chance victim.

Marie is unique among the four victims in that she was the only child who was not asphyxiated. She was also the first of the four children to be killed and the only one to be cut. It seems reasonable to assume that the scene of her death was very bloody. Was dealing with so much blood a problem for her killer? What was the purpose of the cut on the child's chest? And was Marie buried and then disinterred and if so, where and why?

According to the newspaper reports of the case, Maggie and Winnie were definitely killed by men but, although statistically more likely to have been a man, Willie's murderer could have been either male or female. When John Starchfield appeared before magistrates, police surgeon Dr Garrett was specifically asked by Starchfield's solicitor 'This murder could have been committed by a woman equally as well as a man?' Garrett's reply was 'I see no reason why it should not have been.' Since Marie was definitely left in the lavatory by a man, there seems to have been a not unreasonable assumption that her murderer was the person who dumped her body, in spite of the insistence of the member of the public at her inquest, who seemed hell bent on trying to convince the jury that Marie was killed by a woman.

Maggie and Winnie were both 'outraged' by their killers thus there appears to be a definite sexual motive for their murders. Marie was not raped or sexually assaulted. If Willie's murder did take place on the train, given the short time window between stations, it could be that his killer simply did not have sufficient opportunity but there was '...no evidence of vice' apparent at Willie's post-mortem examination, which appears to indicate that the motive for his murder was not a sexual one. Although the evidence against John Starchfield was tenuous and he was ultimately acquitted, many people continued to believe that Willie was killed by his father because he resented paying maintenance for him to his estranged wife. Another prevalent theory was that Willie was killed by someone trying to exact revenge on his father for his intervention in the Titus murder case.

The bodies of Maggie and Marie were both left in lavatories, while Willie was stuffed under the seat of a train. The bodies of all of the children apart from Winnie were in some way concealed – Marie was wrapped in a blanket and brown paper, Willie pushed under the seat and Maggie left in a locked lavatory cubicle. Winnie's body was left in the open air, although the darkness of the night hid her from public view until dawn broke. Marie's body was definitely moved after death, Winnie was almost certainly moved and there are suggestions that both Maggie and Willie might have been killed elsewhere. One point that doesn't seem to have been considered by the investigating officers is that Maggie and Willie could easily have been killed elsewhere and their bodies placed in a suitcase or a soldier's kit bag, which was then carried discretely through the streets and stations. In all four cases, items belonging to the victims were missing, perhaps just mislaid or possibly taken by the murderer as a souvenir. Maggie's hat was never found, neither were Winnie's scout pole or her picture of flags, Marie's religious medal, or the 'To Let' cards that Willie was known to have in his possession when he disappeared.

The circumstances of Winnie's abduction are known, since it was witnessed by her two friends. However, we can only speculate what happened to Maggie, Marie and Willie. All three were taken from public places in broad daylight thus it seems logical to assume that none made any undue protest or fuss. It also suggests that the children initially went willingly with their killers, since any resistance would have almost certainly have attracted the attention of passers-by. It seems likely that the children's abductors were all local to, or at least very familiar with the areas where the children were taken.

The one thing that all four murders definitely had in common was that all of the perpetrators took tremendous risks. (One newspaper printed a suggestion that such was the killer's confidence that he had almost certainly been emboldened by success in committing previous crimes.) In Maggie's and Willie's cases – and most probably Marie's too - the killer made a train journey with either a frightened child in tow or a dead body. Marie's killer boldly walked through the crowded London streets carrying a paper-wrapped package containing a dead child. Winnie's killer seemed to be very familiar with the Woking area and also appeared to know Winnie but, although her two friends said they had seen the man before, unfortunately neither could identify him. Was he confident that Winnie's friends didn't know him or did he take a risk and hope that they wouldn't recognise him? It was reported that when Winnie was abducted '...there were plenty of people about but no one took any notice.' It should be remembered in Winnie's case that she normally attended Nightingale Scouts' meetings with her identical twin sister. Was her killer aware of this and did he deliberately choose a time when Winnie's sister was not with her to seize her? Or, given that the man also asked Doris and Olive to go with him, was Winnie a specific target or would any little girl have served the killer's nefarious

73

purposes? Whichever scenario applies, it seems likely that Winnie's killer knew of some secluded place in the area where he could rape and murder a child without fear of interruption.

'Detectives never allow imagination to overrule solid facts'

In the aftermath of all four murders, there were numerous theories about who might be responsible.

Police investigating Marie Bailes's murder were of the opinion that '...this crime is the work of a madman, who enticed the child away after she left school in Duncan Terrace ... and committed this murder not in South London, where the body was found but in or near Islington'. Having killed Marie in Islington, police believed that she was transported from the Angel of Islington Station to the Elephant and Castle, where her body was left.

Dr Lyttleton Stewart Forbes Winslow, a controversial psychiatrist of the time, described in the contemporary newspapers as '...the great mental specialist', wrote to Scotland Yard with his views on Marie's murder.

The doctor first came to the notice of the public because of his outspoken views on the infamous London 'Jack the Ripper' murders of 1888. He became convinced that he knew the identity of the killer and told the newspapers that, if he was given the assistance of six police constables, he could catch the elusive Ripper for them.

Such were his boasts in the popular press, and subsequently in his memoirs that Forbes Winslow was visited by a senior investigator to test the veracity of his claims. The doctor backpedalled and was quick to insist that he had been misreported and that reporters had tricked him into giving his opinion on the murders. Yet in his letter to Scotland Yard in 1908, he repeated his claims about the Ripper murders and reiterated that, solely because of the publication of his personal knowledge of the facts about the killer's identity, the Ripper had immediately ceased his murderous spree.

Now, Forbes Winslow was eager to offer his views on the murder of Marie Bailes. 'In my opinion, the perpetrator of such crimes is a dangerous homicidal lunatic, now at large. I believe that he could easily be run to earth, were the proper steps taken. I have investigated this late affair (I allude to the Islington tragedy), have interviewed the fellow children and heard their contradictory accounts of some imaginary person who was stated to have been seen hanging about the school yard.

I am of the opinion that the real murderer was not the person who deposited the parcel. I also believe that a little common sense, out of the usual red tape-ism and the regarding the murder of a different type and therefore requiring different plans of investigation from ordinary crimes, that there would be not the least difficulty in capturing without further delay the actual murderer.' Forbes Winslow ended his letter 'Beyond this, I have no intention of saying further in the matter. In trying to capture a murderous lunatic, different plans must be adopted to those which would be adopted in capturing an ordinary criminal.'

As far as the murder of Willie Starchfield was concerned, it was initially widely believed that the boy was killed as revenge for his father's part in the capture and arrest of Titus. A newspaper correspondent, identified only as '...a man who has assisted in unravelling many crimes in the Metropolis in days gone by', stated 'After all, there was a peculiar brotherhood among the criminal foreigners, whose methods of working, especially when it came to a question of revenge, were known only to themselves. In wreaking revenge on a father by means of depriving him of his only child, there was that refinement of cruelty peculiar to the foreign temperament, while the way in which all traces of the murder had been covered up might be taken as strong evidence of premeditation and preparedness.'

Sims (author's collection)

Police quickly discounted the theory that the motive for Willie's murder was revenge, particularly after hearing from journalist, social reformer and writer George Robert Sims, who devoted the later years of his life to the study of the psychology of crime.

Sims felt that it was highly improbable that Willie was killed by a man. Pointing out that the murder was essentially without motive Sims maintained that the only man who could possibly commit such a crime would be a maniac. That being the case, Sims believed that Willie's injuries should have been much more severe.

'As it is, the child looks as though he is asleep' Sims pointed out to a reporter from the *London Evening News*. 'If the boy had been murdered by a maniac, it is probable, almost certain, that the face would have been horribly injured. His tongue, for example, would most likely have been forced out of his mouth. Thus it seems improbable that the boy was murdered by a full grown man. The minimum of force was used.'

'Who, then, did commit the murder?' Sims mused, before answering his own question. 'In my opinion, a moral imbecile, a mental defective, an abnormal boy or youth of fifteen or sixteen and most likely coming from a family with a neurotic history. The case of Willie Starchfield is a case of child murder by a child who was a playmate of the dead boy.'

In the light of what was known about Willie's last movements, Sims's theory is highly plausible. Willie was known to have 'disappeared' once before, returning home late and saying that he had been to the cinema with a bigger boy. Although he wasn't taken very seriously at the time, Angelo Portinari told the police that he had seen Willie with an older boy, who was only slightly taller than him and, of course, if Willie had already made the acquaintance of an older boy, he was more likely to go off with him willingly than to allow a stranger to take him away.

In respect of Winnie Baker's murder, there were very few published theories about the type of man who killed her, other than that he was believed to have been very familiar with the Woking area, where the murder took place.

As far as Maggie Nally's death is concerned, there were numerous theories advanced by both the police and the amateur criminologists of the time. Although it was quickly concluded that Maggie had been killed by a man, early reports stated 'Police are quite alive to the possibility that the murderer might have been dressed in women's clothes'.

It was suggested that the murderer might well suffer from epilepsy but would still be capable of planning his crime and of taking such precautions necessary to evade capture. Such men normally killed at intervals and, according to the experts and medical criminologists of the time, it was not impossible for them to forget their crimes and become totally unaware that '… they have the blood guilt upon them'. 'In other words', explained one contemporary newspaper 'the brain is so constituted that they quite forget they are criminals until another attack comes on.'

Basing his conclusions on published facts, one criminologist was certain that Maggie knew her murderer, even if only as a casual acquaintance as he believed that, as a rule, children of her age did not go off with strangers willingly. 'Such an assumption justifies the belief that Maggie's killer either lived near her home or near the homes of her relatives around Carlisle Street' he explained. The criminologist narrowed down the suspects to someone who either lived or worked in the Harrow Road or Edgware Road areas, adding that he would almost certainly know Aldersgate Street Station very well, probably using the station regularly, travelling backwards and forwards and passing the scene of his crime every day. This observation ties in with what we know about Offender Profiling today. Crimes are most likely to occur in an area in which the perpetrator feels comfortable and with which he or she is familiar in non-criminal life (Rossmo, 2000). There is therefore a very strong possibility that Maggie's killer lived, worked or had close familial connections with the area around Carlisle Street.

Working on the assumption that Maggie knew her killer, it is also possible that she met up with a man in uniform and genuinely believed that he was somebody that she knew, for example, one of her uncles. Recent research has shown that whereas relatively young children are good at recognising faces, their ability to do so is severely hampered when the person is wearing a hat. Since the soldier that Maggie was supposedly with on the bus was said to be wearing a uniform and cap, it is very possible that the man's clothing may have confused her and caused a case of mistaken identity.

Finally, reported sightings of Maggie with a soldier led to speculation that her killer was somebody who was on home leave from the front. A report in the *Manchester Evening News* read: 'The strain of the trenches is so great that a certain number of men in both the German and the Allied armies give way under the strain. For these unhappy men, asylums have to be provided but it is quite possible that in isolated cases a man mentally deranged by the tremendous strain and stress of the trenches may escape medical notice and get back on leave. As this terrible crime is almost certainly the crime of a maniac, this consideration is one that is bound to be weighed.'

'Let him do one manly thing while he lives'.

The inquest on Maggie Nally's death concluded on 22 April with a verdict by the jury of wilful murder against some person or persons unknown and coroner Waldo notified the Registrar, who officially recorded the cause of death as 'Found dead on 4 April 1915, Aldersgate Street Station. Cause of Death: Asphyxia by a gag in her mouth and syncope from *status lymphaticus* when she was outraged and violated'. Before the inquest was formally closed, Detective Inspector Thompson paid tribute to the press on behalf of the police, saying that they had been of great assistance to them at every stage of their search for the killer. However, according to Thompson, the problem that the investigating officers were faced with was a complete dearth of any real clues on which to work and thus when Maggie Nally's funeral took place on 26 April 1915, they were no nearer to finding her killer than they had been on the day of her murder.

It was said that around forty thousand men, women and children lined the streets to watch the cortege and indeed Father Worsley, who conducted the funeral service, commented in his address 'The whole of London seems to have turned out to show them [the Nally family] some respect.'

The coffin, bearing a pillow of white flowers from Maggie's parents and a wreath from her last playmate Alice Scott, was carried from the house in Amberley Road to the hearse for its final journey to Kensal Green by four corporals of the Army Service Corps from Woolwich. The soldiers came at the instigation of Corporal Griffin, a relative of the Nally family, because they wanted to '...show the sympathy of the A. S. C. and the resentment of the army at the slur which has been cast upon them by the allegation that a soldier had been responsible for the crime.'

The Nallys were almost overwhelmed by the tremendous outpouring of public sympathy, which manifested itself in numerous wreaths and other tokens of sympathy, many of which came from serving soldiers. A private in the Northumberland Fusiliers sent a pencil sketch of Maggie to her parents, while another soldier wrote to them enclosing money for a wreath with a message that he hoped that '…the man who has struck you such an awful blow will speedily be brought to book.'

This sentiment was echoed by Father Worsley. 'Oh, that that man could have seen the tears of the multitude this afternoon as we passed along! He must have had a heart of stone if he were not moved.' Worsley appealed to the murderer 'Let him do one manly thing while he lives. At any rate, let him give himself up and atone for what he has done and accepting the punishment of the law, die as a man. What a conscience he must have! How can he go about? Almighty God will punish him most severely if he does not make repentance here.' Sadly, nobody's conscience was sufficiently troubled to induce a confession.

In the days following the murder, thirty-four-year-old former soldier Thomas Kenny was arrested for trying to inveigle his way into a house in Carlisle Street. Kenny, who was discharged from the Army after a period of imprisonment for theft, knocked on a door in Carlisle Street, which was opened by eight-year-old Ada Hooper. Kenny proceeded to question Ada about how old she was, whether her mother and father were in (both were out), if she went to school and what time her mother would be home. When Ada had innocently answered all of the questions to his satisfaction, Kenny walked into the house, closing the door behind him.

Luckily, a woman living upstairs heard what was happening and ran down to eject him from the house. At that moment, Ada's mother returned and summoned a policeman, to whom Kenny was handed over.

At Marylebone Police Court, on 8 May 1915, Kenny swore that, being desperate for money, he merely wanted to see if he could find some clothes to pawn. He was remanded in custody while the police investigated further. Two of the detectives investigating Maggie Nally's murder were present at the court hearing but it has proved impossible to find any further reports of Kenny's criminal career, so he was presumably eliminated from the murder enquiry.

On 20 March 1916, Manchester police arrested a man following allegations made against him as a consequence of a domestic argument. City of London police interviewed the suspect and were satisfied that he had nothing whatsoever to do with Maggie Nally's murder. He was released without charge.

Although Spilsbury's diagnosis of *status lymphaticus* was in line with the medical knowledge of the day, it could arguably have had far reaching consequences on any subsequent enquiries into Maggie Nally's murder.

Three years earlier in 1912, Spilsbury conducted a post-mortem examination on twenty-six-year-old Alice Rosina Balsdon (or Balsden), a.k.a. 'Bristol Dolly', who was found dead at Blenheim Mansions, Shroton Street, Marylebone, on 28 February of that year.

Spilsbury noted a number of marks on the dead woman's throat, in particular ten distinct impressions in the flesh near her Adam's apple, which he believed had been caused by somebody's fingernails. 'There was a considerable amount of haemorrhage in the muscles of the upper part of the front of the neck' stated the pathologist, caused by what he deemed 'considerable pressure' on the dead girl's throat. Even so, Spilsbury ruled that death was due to asphyxia, caused by throttling, while the victim was suffering from the condition of *status lymphaticus.*

Under questioning, Spilsbury forwarded his opinion that, if Dolly had not suffered from the condition, the pressure on her neck alone would most probably not have been sufficient to cause her death. His conclusions were supported by Dr E. A. Boyd, who attributed the main cause of Dolly's death to *status lymphaticus,* '... a condition which rendered a person liable to sudden death upon the slightest shock.'

Dr A. J. Pepper completely disagreed. An advisor to the Director of Public Prosecutions, he was certain that the pressure on the victim's neck was sufficient to have killed her in a very short time, even without *status lymphaticus*. Thus, when Dolly's lover Maurice Cecil Alabaster (a.k.a. Portalis) was charged with her wilful murder, the crux of the proceedings against him boiled down to the diametrically opposing views of the medical witnesses.

According to the prosecution Alabaster was living off Dolly's earnings (She was euphemistically described as 'an actress' but was almost certainly a prostitute.) On the evening of Dolly's death, neighbours living in the block of flats heard two sharp, staccato screams, followed by silence from Dolly's apartment and the following day, she was found dead in her bed, by which time. Alabaster had already fled to France, where he was later arrested in Paris.

At twenty-three-year-old Alabaster's subsequent trial at the Old Bailey, he was charged with both wilful murder and manslaughter. His defence counsel, Mr Marshall Hall testified that his client was '...a man of little or no mental calibre', who was classed as an abnormal child and was removed from several schools by his father at the request of his teachers. When he met Dolly Balsdon, it was love at first sight for both of them yet her infatuation with him resulted in intense jealousy. Nevertheless, although he was already married to someone else, Alabaster was smitten and the couple set up home together in the flat in Blenheim Mansions.

Although living off Dolly's earnings, Alabaster later insisted that he wanted her to give up her immoral lifestyle, and had arranged to marry her and start a new life in a tobacconist's business. On the night of February 27, a row broke out between Dolly and her fiancé, after she accused him of over familiarity with a girl living in the flat above. In a rage, Dolly threatened to leave and began dressing in order to do so. Attempting to prevent her from going, Alabaster seized her by the shoulder and throat, at which, according to him, she screamed twice and fell back dead.

Alabaster firmly denied any intention to kill Dolly, or even to do her harm and, on the advice of his counsel, pleaded guilty to manslaughter at his trial. Mr Justice Bankes directed the jury to return a formal verdict of guilty of manslaughter and Alabaster was sentenced to just nine months in prison.

The newspapers of the time detail many similar cases of murder victims, who were suspected on post-mortem examination of suffering from *status lymphaticus.* Most of the murderers in such cases were either found not guilty or deemed guilty of the lesser offence of manslaughter and given very short sentences, on the grounds that there were no outward signs of the condition and therefore a killer could not possibly be aware that his / her victim was liable to almost literally drop dead at the slightest sign of aggravation. This state of affairs continued for many years, even after the very existence of the condition had been disproved following the research by the Medical Research Council and Pathological Society of Great Britain and Ireland in 1931.

In 1943, twenty-seven-year-old soldier Allan Dennis Witcomb of Hingeston Street, Birmingham appeared at Birmingham Assizes, charged on his own confession with the murder of his two-year-old niece, Doreen Frances Bradley ten years earlier on 10 March 1933. Witcomb told police that, while Doreen was asleep in bed, he pulled the bedclothes over her head and pressed them down on her face.

At the time, a post-mortem examination determined the cause of death as *status lymphaticus* and possible epilepsy and, as a result, the then Birmingham coroner Dr Davidson saw no need for an inquest. On 19 April 1943, when Witcomb eventually confessed to his niece's murder, no evidence was offered against him and he was discharged from court a free man. In 1948, Witcomb was implicated in the murder of a neighbour, sixty-nine-year-old widow Harriet Mills, of Hingeston Street. Even though pathologist Professor J. M. Webster had testified that the cause of death was 'manual constriction of the neck', this time the jury returned a verdict of accidental death and Witcomb again avoided charges.

In 1950, there was another almost identical murder. Fifty-seven-year-old widow Elsie Ivy Aston also lived on Hingeston Street and police routinely interviewed all of her neighbours. When they got to Witcomb, he immediately confessed to murdering both Mrs Mills and Mrs Aston, saying that he felt compelled to kill whenever there was a full moon. In July 1950, the jury at the Birmingham Assizes found him guilty but insane and ordered him to be detained during the King's pleasure. He was sent to Broadmoor Criminal Lunatic Asylum.

Although Maggie Nally's murderer was initially vigorously pursued by the police, tragically, her death came only weeks before the first of many German air raids on London. By the last air raid in October 1917, an estimated two hundred people in the capital had lost their lives, many more had been maimed and injured, not to mention the catastrophic damage to property and immense disruption to the daily routines of those who lived and worked in the capital. At the same time, police officers countrywide had to contend with depleted manpower, as officers left the force to serve their country, which led to cancelled leave and unpaid overtime, causing those remaining officers to be overworked and also to feel demoralised. By 1916, a police constable of twenty years' experience could expect to be paid less than an unskilled labourer and many were forced to take 'backhanders' or face starvation. Although many more Special Constables were recruited and given greater powers during WW1, their main role was the maintenance of public order rather than crime detection.

It therefore stands to reason that police priorities may well have changed with the advent of air raids on London, particularly if the investigating officers considered that Maggie's killer might conceivably get off very lightly if caught in view of Spilsbury's diagnosis of *status lymphaticus*. The fact that the child was supposedly seen with a soldier could have fostered the view that her killer would probably be leaving the country shortly, if he hadn't already left, thus effectively removing any threat to the safety of other children. With the murders of Marie Bailes, Willie Starchfield, Winnie Baker and Maggie Nally, such was the complete dearth of clues and the lack of evidence for police to work on that in each case there seems to be a sense that detectives were waiting for the killer to strike again in the hope that this time he would slip up and reveal his identity. Maggie's was the last murder of the four and there do not seem to have been any comparable murders after hers in the London area - whether any or all of the other three murders were committed by her killer is questionable.

Afterword:

After the death of their eldest daughter, John Henry and Christine Nally were left with three surviving children, Sydney Thomas Walker Nally, John Patrick Nally and Ellen F. Nally. The couple went on to have Kathleen Mary Nally (1916), Patrick Arthur Nally (1921), Christine Mary Nally (1925) and Elsie J. Nally (1928).

Of the Nallys' eight offspring, four died tragically young. Aside from Maggie's untimely death, Elsie died aged one, Ellen died aged twenty-four and Sydney was killed aged thirty-three, while fighting in the Second World War.

John Henry Nally died in 1928 at the age of fifty-one, while his wife survived until 1970 when she died aged eighty-five. According to one of her descendants, she kept a picture of Maggie on the wall of her flat until her death.

Bibliography:

Newspapers:

Birmingham Mail

City Press

Clerkenwell Daily Chronicle

Daily Chronicle

Daily Express

Daily Mail

Daily Mirror

Dundee Courier

Evening Standard

Guardian / Manchester Guardian

London Evening News

Manchester Courier

Manchester Evening News

Observer

Pall Mall Gazette

Sunday Post

Times

Western Times

Articles, Books, Journals and Magazines:

Dally, A, (1997), Status Lymphaticus: Sudden Death in Children from 'Visitation of God' to Cot Death, *Medical History, Vol 41 pp. 70-85*

Douglas, J. E. (2010) *Why killers take trophies,* Mindhunters Inc.

Freire A. and Lee, K. (2001) Face recognition in 4- to 7-year-olds: processing of configural, featural, and paraphernalia information. *Journal of Experimental Child Psychology, Vol 80 pp347 - 371*

Furedi, Frank (2008) *Paranoid Parenting,* London, Continuum International Publishing Group Ltd

Guntheroth, W. G. (1993), The Thymus; Suffocation and Sudden Infant Death Syndrome – Social Agenda or Hubris, *Perspect Biol Med 1993, Vol 37, pp. 2-13* in Jacobs, M.T., Frush, D.P. Donnelly, L.F. (1999), The Right

Place at the Wrong Time: Historical Perspective of the Relation of the Thymus Gland and Paediatric Radiology, Radiology 1999, Vol 210, pp11-16

Hicks J. and Allen G. (1999), *A Century of Change: Trends in UK Statistics since 1900,* London, House of Commons Library

Jacobs, M.T., Frush, D.P. Donnelly, L.F. (1999), The Right Place at the Wrong Time: Historical Perspective of the Relation of the Thymus Gland and Paediatric Radiology, *Radiology 1999, Vol 210, pp11-16*

Mitchell, S, ed. (1988) *Victorian Britain: An Encyclopaedia,* London and New York, Routledge

Osler, W. (1898) *The Principles and Practice of Medicine,* 3rd edition, Edinburgh and London, Young J. Pentland.

Rossmo, D. K. (2000). *Geographic profiling,* Boca Raton, Florida: CRC Press

Weller, K. *'Don't be a soldier: The radical anti-war movement in North London 1914-1918'*

Printed in Great Britain
by Amazon

36972375R00051